C000173796

100 WALKS IN
Staffordshire

The Crowood Press

First published in 1992 by
The Crowood Press Ltd
Ramsbury
Marlborough
Wiltshire SN8 2HR

© The Crowood Press Ltd 1992

British Library Cataloguing-in-Publication Data
A catalogue record for this book is
available from the British Library

All maps by Sharon Perks

Cover picture by John Cleare

Typeset by Carreg Limited, Nailsea, Bristol

Printed in Great Britain by Redwood Press Ltd, Melksham, Wilts

THE CONTRIBUTORS

Trevor Antill

David Bishop

R. Gilbody

Jeff Kent

Bill McGill

E. A. Parkes

Barrie Robertson

CONTENTS

36. Circuit of Rudyard Lake 5m (8km)
37. Wrottesley Park 5m (8km)
38. Okeover, Blore and Coldwall Bridge 5m (8km)
39. Rushton Spencer and Gun End 5m (8km)
40. Haughton and Berry Ring 5m (8km)
41. Milldale, Stanshope and Alstonefield 5m (8km)
42. Six Lane Ends and Turner's Pool 5m (8km)
43. Calf Heath and Shareshill 5m (8km)
44. Betley and Heighley 5m (8km)
45. Farley, Longshaw and Ramshorn 5m (8km)
46. Madeley and Aston 5m (8km)
47. Upper Longdon and Flaxley Green 5m (8km)
48. The Carry Lane Track 5m (8km)
49. The Caldon Valley 5m (8km)
50. Wetley Rocks and Consalldale 5m (8km)
51. The 'Ha-Ha' Walk $5^1/_2$m (9km)
52. Tixall and Hanyards $5^1/_2$m (9km)
53. Swinscoe and Stanton $5^1/_2$m (9km)
54. Gnosall and Shelmore Wood 6m (9.5km)
55. Ramshorn and the Weaver Hills 6m (9.5km)
56. Shareshill and Laches 6m (9.5km)
57. Denstone and Alton 6m (9.5km)
58. Abbots Castle and Trysull 6m (9.5km)
59. Kingsley and Booth's Hall 6m (9.5km)
60. Denford and Wall Grange $6^1/_4$m (10km)
61. Alstonefield and Hall $6^1/_2$m (10.5km)
62. Oakamoor and Hawksmoor Woods $6^1/_2$m (10.5km)
63. The Manifold Way $6^1/_2$m (10.5km)
64. Alton and the Churnet Valley $6^1/_2$m (10.5km)
65. Ellastone, Wootton and Stanton $6^1/_2$m (10.5km)
66. Hilderstone and Leigh $6^3/_4$m (11km)
67. Middle Mayfield and Stanlow 7m (11km)
68. Weeford 7m (11km)
69. Leek and Morridge Edge 7m (11km)
70. Wetton Mill, Butterton and Warslow 7m (11km)
71. Cannock Chase 7m (11km)
72. Freehay and Threapwood 7m (11km)

INTRODUCTION

The Crowood Press are greatly indebted to the contributors who walked cheerfully all over the county researching the walks for this book. It must be borne in mind that while all the details of these walks (hedges, fences, stiles, and so on) were correct at the time of going to print, the countryside is constantly changing and we cannot be held responsible if details in the walk descriptions are found to be inaccurate. We would be grateful if walkers would let us know of any major alterations to the walks described so that we may incorporate any changes in future editions. Please write to THE 100 WALKS SERIES, The Crowood Press, Crowood Lane, Ramsbury, Marlborough, Wiltshire SN8 2HR. Walkers are strongly advised to take with them the relevant map for the area and Ordnance Survey maps are recommended for each walk. The walks are listed by length - from approximately 3 miles to 14 miles. No attempt has been made to estimate how long the walks will take as this can vary so greatly depending on the strength and fitness of the walkers and the time spent exploring the points of interest highlighted. Nearly all the walks are circular and the majority offer a recommended place to seek refreshments. Telephone numbers of these pubs and cafés are included in case you want to check on opening times, meals available, and so on.

We hope you enjoy exploring the county of Staffordshire in the best possible way - on foot - and ask that you cherish its beautiful places by always remembering the country code:

Enjoy the country and respect its life and work
Guard against all risk of fire
Fasten all gates
Keep dogs under close control
Keep to public footpaths across all farmland
Use gates and stiles to cross field boundaries
Leave all livestock, machinery and crops alone
Take your litter home
Help to keep all water clean
Protect wildlife, plants and trees
Make no unnecessary noise

Good walking.

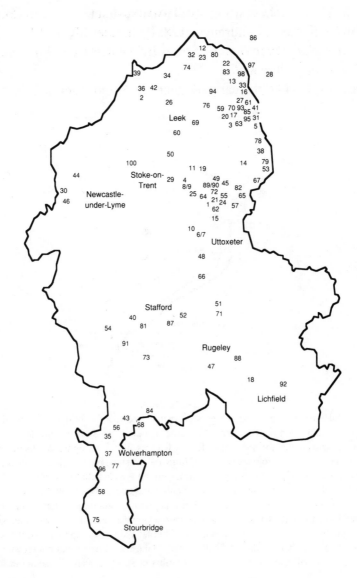

86

12
32 23 80
74   22
                83 98
                13 33
94   16
        76 59 70 93 27 61 41
Leek   20 17 85 31
        69   3 63 95 5
60

39
36 42
2
26

97
28

78
38
79
53
67

50
100
11 19
Stoke-on-   29 4   49
Trent   8/9 89/90 45 82
            25 64 72 55 65
                1 21 24 57
                62
                15

14

44
30
46
Newcastle-
under-Lyme

10
6/7   Uttoxeter
48
66

51
Stafford   71
40   52
54 81 87
91
73   Rugeley
47
18
92
Lichfield

88

43 84
56 68
35
37 Wolverhampton
96 77
58
75   Stourbridge

Walk 1   OAKAMOOR AND DIMMINGSDALE   3m (5km)

Maps: OS Sheets Landranger 128; Pathfinder SK 04/14.

A flat path through banks of trees by the River Churnet makes this a good family walk.

Start: At 053447, the car park near the Admiral Jervis Inn.

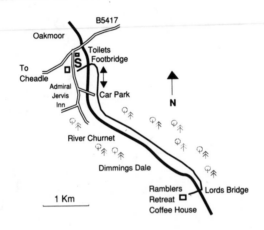

From the car park, go across the grassed picnic area to a footbridge over the river. Canoeists can often be seen here. This area is a credit to Staffordshire Moorlands Council who created the picnic area from what was Bolton's Copper Works in 1962. The stone gate pillars from the railway sidings and the stone bases for heavy machinery can still be seen. Cross the bridge and turn right on a wide path to a second car park. This was the site of Oakamoor Railway Station and one of the old platforms can still be seen over on the left. Go to the end of this platform and turn off left on to a path which leads to a stile. Cross on to a wide path which was once the railway line. Keep on this path for about 1½ miles through the Churnet Valley passing first a local cricket field, then a football field, and finally a small lake where fishermen congregate. At the right time of year this walk offers a number of sporting scenes! Watch out for a stone bridge (Lords Bridge) crossing above the path and when about 50 yards from it look out for a plank bridge over the ditch to the left. Cross this to a narrow path leading up to the bridge. Cross the bridge and follow the path through to a minor road. The Ramblers Retreat Coffee House (which has been converted from a hunting lodge) is opposite where refreshments may be taken either inside or out in the garden.

The return is back the way you came – across the bridge and back along the Churnet Valley to Oakamoor.

REFRESHMENTS:
The Ramblers Retreat (tel no: 0538 702730).
The Admiral Jervis Inn, Oakamoor (tel no: 0538 702187).

Walk 2   **RUDYARD AND HORTON**   3m (5km)

Maps: OS Sheets Landranger 119; Outdoor Leisure 24.

A delightful and scenic short walk for all the family. Horton is particularly charming.

Start: At 955579, the Rudyard car park situated on the old railway embankment.

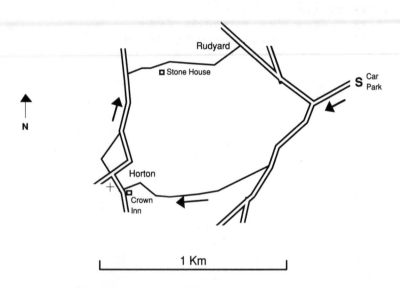

Go down to the road and turn left for the village centre. At the Poachers Tavern take the left-hand turn and walk for 300m to the end of the built-up area and the speed limit sign. At this point go up a lane and footpath, right, to cross a stile by a fingerpost to Horton. Follow the obvious footpath over stiles towards Horton. Soon the Crown Inn and church come into view, situated on the hill in the delightful hamlet of Horton. Cross a small stream and head up the bank, keeping the hedgerow on your left. At the lane leave the field through a gate. You can go left here for refreshment at the Crown Inn.

To continue, go right alongside the churchyard to a road junction. Go straight across and diagonally right up a small lane past a magnificent old vicarage. Go ahead on a lane (footpath). After 150m, at a stile, turn down the field to the right to reach a squeezer and single stone slab footbridge. Cross these and head up the field alongside the road, following a hedgerow, until it is possible to leave by a stile on to the road. Turn left for 250m and at a footpath sign go right along a farm lane to Stone House. Continue in the same direction for 300m, past old quarries in a wood, to reach a road. Turn right here to go through **Rudyard** and back to the car park.

POINTS OF INTEREST:
Rudyard – A Victorian inland resort that is enjoying a new lease of life. Kipling's parents reputedly named him after happy memories of this place.

REFRESHMENTS:
The Poachers Tavern, Rudyard (tel no: 053833 208)
The Crown Inn, Horton (tel no: 053833 275)

Walk 3   DIMMINGSDALE AND OUSAL DALE   3m (5km)

Maps: OS Sheets Landranger 119; Pathfinder SK 04/14.

A fine rugged stroll up and round the sandstone and Bunter pebble beds of the deeply incised Churnet Valley.

Start: At 062432, The Rambler's Retreat café.

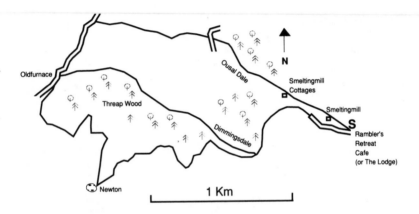

Continue past the car park along a narrow metalled road and, after a little way, take a left turn. Continue to an obvious arched bridge. Just past this turn right to find the start, by the Ramblers Retreat Café, or The Lodge as it is marked on the OS map.

Take the right-hand footpath past the fishponds and remains of the **smelting mill** to where a house is being renovated. Continue past this up through the charming mixed woodland and rocks of Ousal Dale, crossing an old carriageway to meet a lane. Turn right along this lane past a pond and follow it across several fields to meet a minor road.

Turn left for 400m to a prominent footpath sign at Oldfurnace for Dimmingsdale. A short route back is to take this footpath direct into Dimmingsdale and so back to the start. Alternatively at this sign go up the hill across fields to woodland and on to

Newton. At Newton go left and down to meet the track in Dimmingsdale. Pass numerous fishponds made from the old water storage system for the smelting mill and follow the wide carriageway track back to the start through dense woodland.

POINTS OF INTEREST:
Smelting Mill – An 18th-century lead smelting mill for the ores from Ecton.

REFRESHMENTS:
The Ramblers Retreat Café, (tel no: 0538 702730).

Walk 4   HAWKSMOOR NATURE RESERVE   3m (5km)

Maps: OS Sheets Landranger 119; Pathfinder SK 04/14.

A walk through part of a wooded nature reserve belonging to the National Trust.

Start: At 033438, High Shutt.

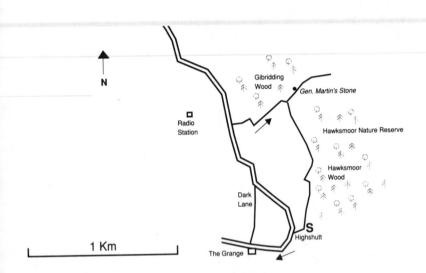

Walk down the road towards Cheadle a short distance to reach The Grange. Opposite a footpath leads across fields and comes out on Dark Lane. Turn left along the lane for about 200 yards to reach a stile on the right. Go over and down through fields towards woodland. Hereabouts it can be muddy following rain. Proceed downwards, keeping Gibridding Wood on your left, and go over the stile into the next field (National Trust property). Continue downwards with woodland still on your left. In the gully by the woodland to the left is **General Martin's Stone**. Walk straight up to the corner of the narrowing field where there is a stile into the woodland. Follow the path up to the top of the wood. Here the ascent is extremely steep. Once at the top, keep to the path which follows the fence on your right. As you walk along it there are good views down over the **Hawksmoor Nature Reserve** to your left. Keep to this path, with the fence on your right, and in less than $^1/_4$ mile it will bring you to the B5417 road near to the start.

POINTS OF INTEREST:

General Martin's Stone – The stone was erected to the memory of General William Reid Martin who died on the spot following a fall from his horse on December 31st 1892.

Hawksmoor Nature Reserve – A fine reserve created during the late 1920's at the suggestion of J R B Masefield. A plaque at the main entrance gates, which was placed there a few years after the creation of the reserve, records his keen interest and great love for the natural history of the area.

Walk 5   ECTON COPPER MINES   3m (5km)

Maps: OS Sheets Landranger 119; Outdoor Leisure 24.

A pleasant family walk skirting early industrial remains.

Start: At 103593, the Peak District Car Park at Hulme End near Hartington.

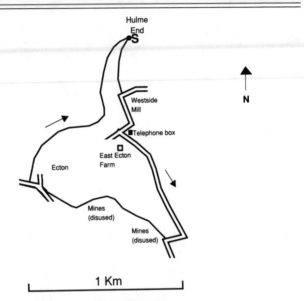

Leave the car park along the smooth-surfaced **Manifold Trail** for about 150m, then go left over a stile and diagonally right across a field to another stile in the boundary fence. Head in a similar direction to a footbridge over the **River Manifold**. Cross the footbridge to a road and farm. Go right along the road for about 300m, following the river, then turn left by a cottage to pass a telephone box along a lane signposted for Back of Ecton. Follow the lane past a fishpond and a boathouse where the road bends sharply right and uphill. After 100m go right up a lane that contours the hillside rising gradually to a squeezer by old **mineshafts**. *

Go through the squeezer – there are good views all round at this point – and take the field boundary down the hill to a stile in a wall by some buildings. The hillside here is rich in wild flowers. The landslip on your left is a result of ancient mining.

Go over the stile and turn right down the lane past the magnificent Gothic pile and down to the road. Cross the road and pick up the Manifold Track again that will take you back to the car park.

*NB In this area great care must be exercised in the control of youngsters and dogs as the mineshafts are inadequately fenced, keen or inquisitive children and animals could fall down the gaping holes.

POINTS OF INTEREST:
The Manifold Trail – Formed along the track of the old Manifold Light Railway this excellent footpath for wheelchairs was constructed in 1937 by a far sighted Staffordshire County Council. Bicycles can be hired for the 7 mile valley walk/ride.
Mineshafts – These deep shafts are part of the derelict Ecton Mines closed in 1873, but once the largest in Europe. Do not enter any tunnels, they are in a dangerous condition.
River Manifold – This fascinating river does a disappearing trick further down the valley and reappears several miles downstream.

REFRESHMENTS:
The Manifold Valley Hotel, (tel no: 029884 537).

Walks 6 & 7 **HOLLINGTON LEVEL** $3^{1}/_{2}$m (5.5km) or 2m (3km)
Maps: OS Sheets Landranger 128; Pathfinder SK 04/14 & 03/13.
A walk over fields and country roads. The going is fairly easy.
Start: At 036398, by the unclassified Cheadle to Hollington road.

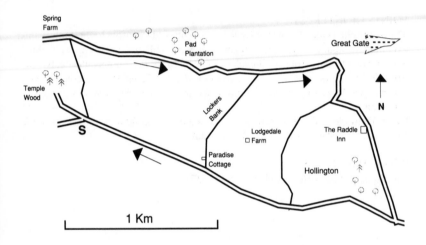

Across the road from the parking area a stile leads into a field. From here the Weavers Hills are seen ahead and in the distance. They form the southern end of the Pennine Chain. Walk down the field to the Winnoth Dale to Great Gate road and turn right along it towards Great Gate. In spring and summer lovely birdsong may be heard in the woodland to the left of this lane. About $^{1}/_{2}$ mile along it Locker's Bank joins from the right but you keep straight ahead and soon come to the small village of **Great Gate.** On entering the village turn right by the public telephone and proceed up the lane towards Hollington but at the first sharp corner (100 yards from the telephone) a public footpath enters fields on the right and leads up the winding, but well-defined, track to the road at the west end of Hollington village. On reaching the road turn right and proceed along it to return to the starting point. This section of road is known as Hollington Level and the Weavers Hills are again in view on the right, while on the

24

opposite side but much further away, The Wrekin in Shropshire and hills in Wales may be seen in exceptionally clear weather. As you walk along the Level a Roman road is running almost parallel with you to the left in nearby fields. Farming has unfortunately meant that no remains of the road are visible in the fields.

For the shorter walk, half-way along the Level the other end of Locker's Bank joins on the right. Use of this effectively cuts the walk in half. If the section involving Great Gate is chosen, the best parking place is by the public telephone.

POINTS OF INTEREST:

Great Gate – It is said the name comes from it having been the 'Great Gate' or main entrance towards Croxden Abbey (ruins in care of English Heritage) and which are situated nearly a mile south of Great Gate.

REFRESHMENTS:

The Raddle Inn, $\frac{1}{4}$ mile up the Hollington lane from Great Gate (tel no: 088926 278).

Walks 8 & 9   **HIGH SHUTT** $3\frac{1}{2}$m (5.5km) or 5m (8km)
Maps: OS Sheets Landranger 119; Pathfinder SK 04/14.
A fine walk through a National Trust Nature Reserve.
Start: At 039443, inside the entrance to the Hawksmoor Nature
Reserve.

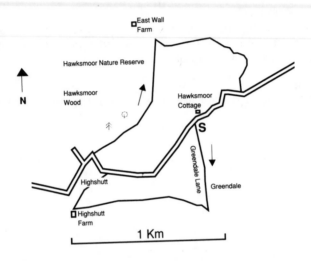

Cross over the B5417 road and go down Green Dale lane for a little over $\frac{1}{4}$ mile, past cottages on the left. Shortly afterwards a stile on the right leads into fields. Cross fields, quickly seeing, High Shutt Farm ahead. The path leads to the farmyard. Once out of the farmyard turn right up a track and following it for $\frac{1}{4}$ mile to reach the B5417. Turn left along the road for about 120 yards, and enter Hawksmoor Nature Reserve (see Note to Walk 4) on the right. Once inside the reserve take the path which leads steeply down towards the middle of the reserve. In $\frac{1}{2}$ mile this path joins a farm track. Near this point there is a large yew tree behind which may be made out the remains of foundations of an old cottage which was occupied until fifty years ago by a lady and gentleman who had a great love for the flora and fauna of the reserve. Turn left down the track in the direction of East Wall Farm but before you reach it turn up the track that branches to the right. Follow this all the way to its junction with the B5417 where you turn right along a road to return to the start..

Note: A very fine, longer, walk can be made by continuing Walk 4 and this Walk. Start as for this walk and follow it to High Shutt. From there follow Walk 4 to General Martin's Stone, but continue to East Wall Farm. There turn south to regain this walk.

Walk 10   GREAT GATE AND BRADLEY   3$\frac{1}{2}$m (5.5km)

Maps: OS Sheets Landranger 128; Pathfinder SK 03/13.

A walk over fields and along country roads.

Start: At 053400, the telephone box in Great Gate.

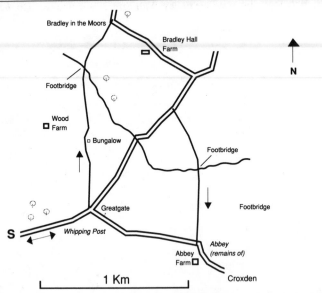

Walk over the ford (footbridge) and through the village in the direction of Alton. At the far end of the village, just where the road to Croxden and Rocester goes off to the right, there is a stone stile in the wall on the left. Go over and up the fields towards Bradley, eventually crossing the farm track that goes up to Wood Farm. Just beyond this the track passes to the left of a bungalow. From this point the small hamlet and church tower of Bradley is seen ahead. The way leads down the field, across the stream then up the fields to Bradley. As you go towards Bradley, Denstone College may be seen in the distance to the right. On reaching the lane at **Bradley** turn right. Go right again at the junction, back in the direction of Great Gate. Not far along the lane (less than $\frac{3}{4}$ mile) a stone stile on the left in a short section of holly hedge gives access to a field. Go across the field, keeping the ditch on your right. At the bottom of the field cross the footbridge and walk about 30 yards up to the corner of the hedge

28

ahead. Go over the stile into the next field and walk up the field with the hedge on your right. At the top of this field you are on a ridge of ground from where, tradition has it, Cromwell's cannons were fired at **Croxden Abbey** during the Civil War. As you go down the field the ruins of Croxden Abbey lie ahead. The ruins are open to the public but if you do not intend to visit them turn right along the road towards Great Gate and return to the starting point by walking back through the village.

POINTS OF INTEREST:

Bradley – The church was built in 1750 and stands on the site of an earlier church. In the churchyard, near the church door, is the tomb of Anne Snape whom it is said died of a broken heart. The inscription on the front of the stone records that she died as long ago as March 25th 1307, the only 14th-century stone in the churchyard. The inscription on the reverse of the stone records that her death broke a true lover's knot. Access to churchyard is up the cottage path near it. The church key can be obtained from the nearby cottage.

Croxden Abbey – Dates from 1174 and was occupied by Cistercian monks. The ruins are always open to the public and are in the care of English Heritage. The name Great Gate is said to have originated from it having been the main entrance to the Abbey.

REFRESHMENTS:
The Raddle Inn (tel no: 088926 278).

Walk 11   HARSTON WOOD AND FOXT   3½m (5.5km)

Maps: OS Sheets Landranger 119; Pathfinder SK 04/14.

A walk through woodland and fields and part of the small village of Foxt.

Start: At 026476, the picnic site at the old Froghall Wharf.

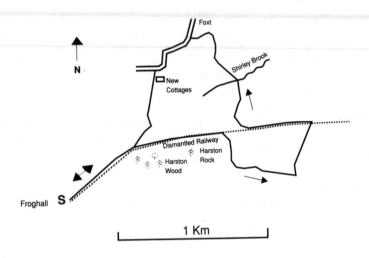

From the picnic site walk up the track of the **dismantled railway** for about ³/₄ mile. The gradient here is gradual and on the way you pass the tall natural column of sandstone called Harston Rock situated on the right, in Harston Wood. About ¹/₄ mile after passing the rock the route leaves the rail track and branches to the right, going through woodland, with a stream on the left. Eventually the path curves round to the left into fields and then returns to the railway track again. On reaching it turn left.

When you come to the stone bridge that passes over the track, walk underneath the bridge and then immediately up the embankment and over the stile by the bridge. The route now crosses the bridge in the direction of Foxt. Go over and down fields and cross Shirley Brook by footbridge. Beyond climb steeply up an old track between stone walls to Foxt. In the village, turn left towards Froghall and after rather more than $^1/_4$ mile a row of cottages is passed on the left. Turn left past the end of the cottages and go steeply down fields to cross Shirley Brook again at another footbridge. Now climb gradually up through the wood to rejoin the old railway track again and go right to return to the starting point after about $^1/_4$ mile.

POINTS OF INTEREST:
Dismantled Railway/Tramway – Built in 1777 to enable horse drawn traffic to haul limestone down to Froghall from the high ground at Cauldon. It was conveyed away from Froghall by canal. The track now forms part of the Staffordshire Moorland Walk.

Walk 12　FLASH AND DUN COW'S GROVE　3³/₄m (6km)

Maps: OS Sheets Landranger 119; Outdoor Leisure 24.

A fairly easy walk with good views of millstone grit hills and valleys.

Start: At 032678, the Travellers' Rest Inn on the A53.

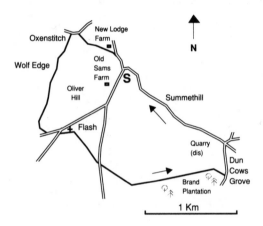

From the pub take the main road north for a short way and then turn first left (signposted to Knotbury). Soon after a road junction to the right, pass the farm at Oxensitch on the left and, immediately beyond, cross a stile on the left. Follow the path ahead uphill, keeping to the right of a hollow and a fence, and gradually bearing right from them. At the right-angle of the fence, go over a stile (which is easily missed) and take the left fork of two faint paths. Follow this diagonally across the field towards a wall, which should be crossed. Continue straight on, with the wall on the right, as the path becomes a track which bends to the left into Flash (the highest village in England). At the road junction turn left, pass The New Inn (where refreshments can be taken) and cross straight over at the next junction, following the path (which is signposted) around the right-hand side of the church. Go through a gate, through a farmyard and follow the gravel track ahead through a second gate towards a track visible at the far side of the main road. Just before a third gate, go over a stile on the left and cross the wall ahead on to the main road. Cross this and take the track almost opposite. Shortly afterwards, bear left as the track forks and cross a stile on the left (which is easily missed) immediately before the first farm building. Go over a second stile on the right almost straight away. Keep on the path to the right of a telegraph pole and aim for the lone tree on the hill ahead. Cross a stream, pass a standing stone (to the left of the lone tree) and go over a stile in the fence ahead. Continue with a wall, then a fence, then an overgrown wall on the right. Walk to the left of Brand Plantation and cross a stile on the right shortly afterwards. This leads down to Dun Cow's Grove. Cross the infant River Manifold and join the road. Turn left on the road and up the hill to a road junction. Turn left here and continue up the hill back to the Travellers' Rest.

REFRESHMENTS:
The Travellers' Rest Inn, Quarnford (tel no: 0298 24253/78704).
The New Inn, Flash (tel no: 0298 22941).

Walk 13   **THE DOVE AND MANIFOLD VALLEYS**   4m (6.5km)
Maps: OS Sheets Landranger 119; Outdoor Leisure 24.
A short and very scenic tour of the two famous Peak District valleys.
Start: At 088649, the car park in Longnor Market.

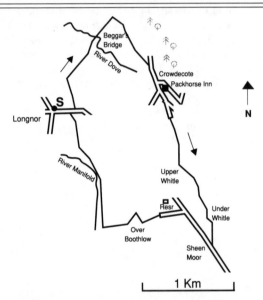

Go east out of the village until you reach the speed limit signs. Here, turn left down a lane and bear right after 200m to head downhill to a barn. At the barn go left, and then immediately right and follow the bridlepath across fields to the **River Dove**. This section can be boggy. Go over the footbridge to some delightful picnic spots. After about 150m turn right over a stile and continue easily to the hamlet of Crowdecote. Pass the Packhorse Inn and then turn left down a lane for 150m. At this point go right down a short lane and cross the River Dove by footbridge. Turn left and follow the fingerposts towards Sheen. This section is over signposted and the farmer is proprietorial! After passing Upper and Under Whittle Farms head up a lane to meet the road. Go right for 0.5km to a left turn just before a water storage reservoir. Go down this lane for about 200m, and at a gate head down the field ahead to exit on the right through another gate. By a water trough turn left down a track to a farm and follow the arrows through the farmyard to leave it by a made-up track. After 100m you will come to a stile set in the middle of nowhere. Cross this heading right and follow the squeezers along the banks of the River Manifold towards Longnor (see Note to Walk 83). There are good picnic spots here, too. Finally head up the slope towards a farm and the village. At the road turn left to regain the Market Place.

POINTS OF INTEREST:
River Dove – This famous river forms the boundary between Staffordshire and Derbyshire, and between gritstone and limestone country.

REFRESHMENTS:
The Cheshire Cheese, Longnor (tel no: 029883 218).
The Crew and Harpur Arms, Longnor (tel no: 029883 205).
The Horseshoe Inn , Longnor (tel no: 029883 262).
The Packhorse Inn, Crowdecote (tel no: 029883 210).

Walk 14   WOOTTON AND THE WEAVER HILLS   4m (6.5km)
Maps: OS Sheets Landranger 119; Pathfinder SK 04/14.

A steady climb to a hill top is rewarded by beautiful and far ranging views.

Start: At 105452, in the Back Lane, beside the Weaver Hills direction sign post.

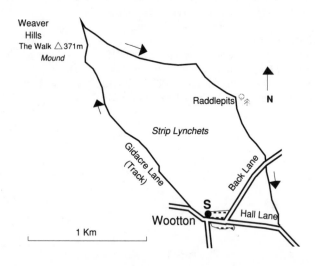

Take the Leek road and just after Show Croft Farm turn right on a rough track (Gidacre Lane). Where the track ends in a field go diagonally left to cross a wall stile. Ascend the field beyond on a line just right of the Trig point to cross a stile in far corner. Go across and round the hillside to a stile by a wall, ignoring one in the wall. After crossing, follow the wall to the corner before continuing slightly left to reach a gate in the corner of the field. The views from the summit are extensive. In the foreground looking south is the JCB complex (earth moving machinery) and to the south west are the Alton Towers leisure complex and the heavily wooded hillsides of the Churnet Valley.

Turn right on a reasonably clear path along the field boundary to reach a stile by a gate. Cross and follow a clear path along field boundaries towards Back Lane. The mound to the right with a tree atop is a tumulus (burial mound), one of several in the vicinity. Stanton village can be seen ahead on the hillside. Descend the lane, passing the humps and hollows of **Raddle Pit** workings, to a 90° bend. Go straight ahead across the stile and down the field to a corner stile and Hall Lane. Go right and follow the lane back to the start.

POINTS OF INTEREST:
Raddle Pits – Used for the extraction of red ochre, a substance used as a colouring pigment.

Walk 15   RAMBLER'S RETREAT TO OLDFURNACE   4m (6.5km)

Maps: OS Sheets Landranger 128; Pathfinder SK 04/14.

This lovely walk goes through woodland and has impressive views of the local valleys.

Start: At 062432, the Rambler's Retreat Café.

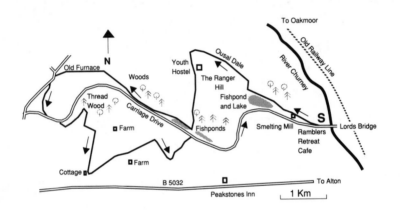

Facing the front of the café, veer over to the right to reach a gradually ascending sandstone track with woods on its right. Pass an old smelting mill, a fishpond and a small lake, all on the left. Where the track forks go to the right and continue upwards following the track round to the left near a farm gate. Eventually you join another path and turn right uphill. At the junction with the Youth Hostel track turn left and pass to the right of the small building. Follow the stone wall on the right. There are fine views of the valley below from here. Cross the memorial stile and follow the path down through the trees to more fishponds. Take the path going right with a stream on your left and go for almost a mile to Oldfurnace.

Turn left on the road, but after about 50 yards go over the stile next to a farm gate on the left. Go diagonally right uphill in a big field, keeping on the left of the gully, to reach a fence. Follow the fence along left, to a stile. Cross on to Carriage Drive – a wide track – and go along it for a few hundred yards until it curves left. There take the path on the right which goes upwards. Follow this path to a stile at the top and cross it into a field. Go along the wall to the right on to farm track. Turn right along the track, with fine views over the Staffordshire Dales. When a cottage is reached on the right, go over a stile by a gate, right, in the corner on the left and cross into a field. Go diagonally across to a stile visible in a wall into a second field and cross to another, visible, stile. In the third field turn right along a wall to a stile in a corner. Cross into a fourth, large, field and go diagonally across it, passing on the right of a large oak tree. Go down to a stile in the right corner, by woods. Cross into a fifth field, keeping to right edge to reach a stile. Cross into woods and follow a gradually descending path. At a fork bear left going more steeply down to reach Carriage Drive again. Turn right and follow this wide track back to the Rambler's Retreat where the walk started.

REFRESHMENTS:
The Rambler's Retreat Café (tel no: 0538 702730).

Walk 16   **HULME END AND BRUND**   4m (6.5km)

Maps: OS Sheets Landranger 119; Outdoor Leisure 24.

An easy walk, mainly along minor roads.

Start: At 102594, the Hulme End car park.

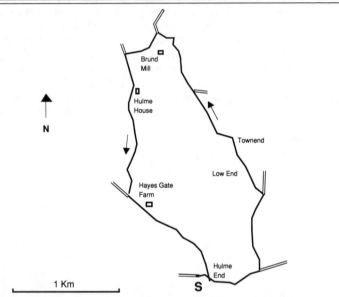

Turn left on to the Manifold Way track and turn right shortly afterwards, at the road junction, on to the B5054. Walk along the road, through Hulme End village, over the River Manifold and up a short, steep hill on the other side. As the incline levels out, take the minor road on the left (signposted to Sheen and Longnor). Follow this downhill, over a stream and up a slope on the other side. Soon afterwards, turn left on to the track to Low End Farm (signposted to Brund). Follow the track through the farmyard, and soon afterwards pass through a gate and continue straight on. The path peters out, but head virtually straight onwards, aiming for the right-hand end of a line of trees and keep a wall on the left. Negotiate another gate, continuing ahead, keeping to the right of a stream running off to the left. Pass through a wall, through two gates in quick succession on to a track and join a minor road. Turn left along this, passing through Brund, and continuing to a road junction. Turn left here (signposted to Hulme

End and Longnor), pass Brund Mill and cross the bridge over the River Manifold. Continue until a road junction and there turn left (signposted to Hulme End). At a further road junction nearly a mile ahead, again turn left (signposted to Hulme End and Hartington) and continue until the B5054 is reached. Turn right on to this and then turn left shortly afterwards on to the Manifold Way and back to the car park.

REFRESHMENTS:
The Manifold Valley Hotel, Hulme End (tel no: 0298 84537).

Walk 17   THE MANIFOLD TRAIL   4m (6.5km)

Maps: OS Sheets Landranger 119; Outdoor Leisure 24.

A relatively easy introduction to the hills and dales found in the Staffordshire area of the Peak National Park.

Start: At 108552, the public car park in Wetton.

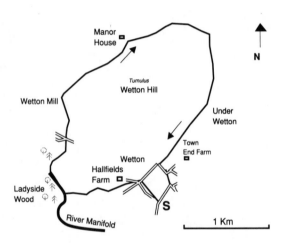

Turn right from the car park, then right again along the lane and left at the T-junction. After a few yards turn left over a wall stile. Turning right to cross the field to a stile in the middle of the far wall. Go over on to a clear path which descends steeply, passing two signed footpaths to Thor's Cave (see Note to Walk 27), to reach the **Manifold Trail** across a footbridge. The river bed may be dry, as for most of the year the River Manifold runs underground from Wetton Mill ($\frac{1}{2}$ mile upstream) before re-surfacing at Ilam, taking 22 hours to cover the 4 miles.

    Continue by turning right along the Trail for an easy, but scenically beautiful, walk to the junction with the road from Wetton coming in from the right. Leave the trail to go straight ahead over a stile into a quiet little valley where the path follows a little stream to a wall stile adjacent to a stone house. This is called Pepper's Inn and as such was used by the miners of Ecton Hill. It is now a private residence. Go over the stile and cross a footbridge before veering left to contour round the lower level of the hill to the far side. The path picks up a boundary wall at a field corner and follows the wall for approximately 300 yards before turning left to a stile. Go over and turn right along a clear, stiled path across fields and past old stone barns to reach Wetton (see Note to Walk 85) at the village street adjacent to a 16th-century farm house. Go down the street and past the pub, turning first right back to the car park a few hundred yards away.

POINTS OF INTEREST:

The Manifold Trail – Runs along the bed of the defunct Leek and Manifold Light Railway (1904–1934) which operated between Waterhouses and Hulme End.

REFRESHMENTS:

The Old Royal Oak, Wetton (tel no: 033527 287).

Maps: OS Sheets Landranger 128; Pathfinder SK 01/11.
A fine walk in the Cannock Chase AONB.
Start: At 045126, the car park at Castle Ring.

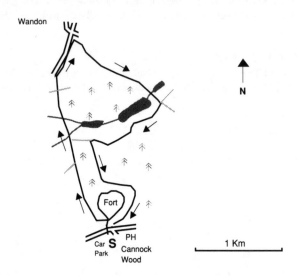

From the car park go through the green kissing gate and on to the ramparts in a clockwise direction. At approximately 9 o'clock a path, in a depression, takes you left into the forest fringe and shortly on to a green forest ride. Go right to a T-junction. Turn left to another junction at a forestry road by overhead wires. Turn right for approximately one mile down into a valley and out up the other side to meet an unclassified road near the Camping and Caravanning Club's Wandon camp site. Here a track runs parallel with the road. Go right on this to reach another forestry road. Go right again, down the valley to a large pool on the right with an overflow going under to the left. Ahead is a junction of forest roads. Turn right and continue, ignoring a branch going to the left.

Now follow a very pleasant walk through mostly coniferous woodlands until you reach a foresters' track cut through the trees on the left. Continuing past this for

50 yards brings you into a dip with a culverted stream. Another 50 yards on is another track on the left, but ignore this and go forward for still another 50 yards and again ignore a track on the left. A 100 yards further there is a track on the right: ignore it! But a further 50 yards again ahead there is a grassy track on the left. Turn on to this and start the climb back up to Castle Ring.

Eventually, emerging on to a graded forest road, turn left until, way in the distance, Rugeley Power Station is visible on your left. Take a path on the right and climb upwards to reach the ramparts of the **Castle Ring Hill Fort** and so back to the car park.

POINTS OF INTEREST:

Castle Ring Hill Fort – Built around 500bc and is a well preserved example covering 9 acres and comprising several ramparts and ditches. The site includes the remains of a much later building, thought to be a medieval hunting lodge associated with the Royal Forest of Cannock Chase. Cannock Chase is one of Britain's finest Areas of Outstanding Natural Beauty (AONB).

REFRESHMENTS:
The Park Gate, Castle Ring (tel no: 0543 682223).

Walk 19   **IPSTONES AND CONSALLFORGE**   4m (6.5km)

Maps: OS Sheets Landranger 119; Pathfinder SK 04/14.

A fairly easy walk through some beautiful woodlands.

Start: At 015497, on the road west from the centre of the village of Ipstones, past a farm on the left and shortly after a right-hand bend.

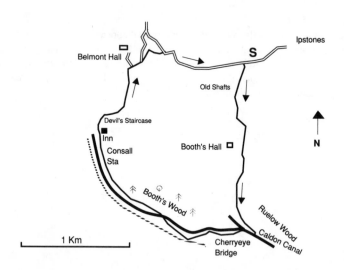

Walk a short distance along the road away from **Ipstones** and turn left down a track. When the track branches, take the left fork and continue through Booth's Hall Farm. Follow the track down the hill. The track becomes a path and passes to the left of a second farm. Continue the descent into the **Churnet Valley** over a stile and cross the bridge over the Caldon Canal. Then turn left and left again on to the canal towpath and back under the bridge. Follow the towpath past a beautiful **bluebell wood** on the opposite bank and carry on until the Black Lion pub at Consallforge (where refreshments may be obtained). Leave the canal here and walk past the front of the pub. Turn right past the toilets and then immediately left to take a path up the side of the valley through a wood. Ascend the two hundred steps of the Devil's Staircase and

46

carry straight on to a stile (which is partly obscured by an overhanging tree) just past a large dip on the right. Cross the stile and turn right at the road ahead. Shortly afterwards, turn right on to a footpath (which is signposted) and descend sixty-six steps. At the bottom of these, follow the path on the left-hand side of a stream in a beautiful wood. Cross the stream and follow the path up to a road. Turn right on to this and follow it back to the start of the walk.

POINTS OF INTEREST:

Ipstones and Ipstones Edge – They are best viewed to advantage during the early stages of the walk.

The Churnet Valley – This heavily-wooded valley is presented at its best on the descent to it from Booth's Hall Farm.

Bluebell wood – There are some delightful bluebell woods en route, especially on the far bank (from the towpath) of the Caldon Canal.

REFRESHMENTS:

The Black Lion Inn, Consallforge (tel no: 0782 550294).

The Lynden Tree, 47 Froghall Road, Ipstones (tel no: 053 876 266370).

The Marquis of Granby, Church Lane, Ipstones (tel no: 053 876 266462).

The Sealion, 41 Brookfield Road, Ipstones (tel no: 053 876 266450).

Walk 20 **FROGHALL WHARF AND HARSTON WOOD** 4m (6.5km)
Maps: OS Sheets Landranger 119; Pathfinder SK 04/14.
A delightful wooded walk through our early industrial past, by fascinating rock formations, and with good spring flowers.
Start: At 025476, the car park at Froghall Wharf.

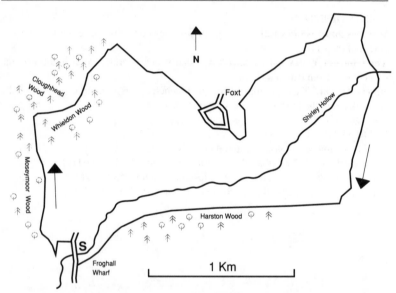

Go over the canal bridge by the **Froghall Wharf** Restaurant and go left and down on to the Cauldon Canal bank. Drop down again to a well-made footbridge. Go over this and up the other side. Turn right along a sometimes muddy track into Moseymoor Wood, following **Blackbank Brook**. The path steepens: take a right fork across the head of an old reservoir dam and keep to the right at the next fork. Continue along the obvious track upwards with the brook on your right. Just beyond some vivid orange mud, stained with limonite, cross another well-made footbridge and go up the bank through Whieldon Wood. Exit at a squeezer and stile and head across fields. Turn right through a gate and stile and then immediately left across fields to a lane and Foxt village. The Fox and Goose pub is up to the left at this point. Go straight over the road along a tarmac lane past a farm. Continue to a narrow walled lane in a wood which

48

goes down to meet another footpath. Go left and over a stile to follow another walled lane up to where it flattens out and joins a footpath. Continue in more or less the same line, passing the top of a wood and taking the top gateway. Head for the first of a series of elegant squeezers across the fields, zig-zagging towards a metalled lane and farm. Follow a sign to Newfields Gallery and pass this to the top of Shirley Hollow. Cross this by a stile and head for Oldridge Pinnacle and farm. At the farm turn right along the **old tramway** passing below Harston Rocks to regain the car park.

POINTS OF INTEREST:
Froghall Wharf – The renovated wharf that used to serve the Cauldon Canal and the inclined tramway.
Blackbank Brook – Apparently named after coal mining operations carried out here long ago.
Old Tramway – The inclined tramway where loaded trucks of limestone used their weight to pull empty trucks to the top. The tramway served the Cauldon Quarries.

REFRESHMENTS:
The Froghall Wharf Restaurant, (tel no: 053871 486).
The Fox and Goose, (tel no: 053871 415).

Walk 21 OAKAMOOR, FARLEY AND THE CHURNET VALLEY 4m (6.5km)

Maps: OS Sheets Landranger 119; Pathfinder SK 04/14.

A walk with fine views over the Churnet Valley and the Farley and Wootton Estates.

Start: At 053448, Oakamoor Picnic site.

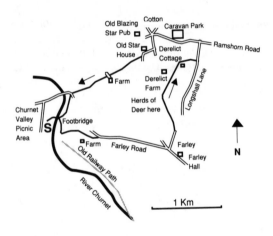

From the Picnic site go across the footbridge and turn right. Go to a log bar, then veer left to a dilapidated kissing gate near the end of one of the old railway platforms. Go through into a field and uphill along the hedge on the left. At the top go through a hedge gap into a field and continue straight ahead. Cross a farm track and veer right to go through a gate (or over a stile) into a field. Go round a low iron railing to a stone wall on the left, and follow it along to a stile on to the road. Turn right and go to T-junction in Farley. Turn right, cross the road, and go up the lane between stone houses to a stile at its end. Cross the stile and follow the path to left (NOT the path straight ahead going downhill). Watch out for herds of deer in the fields from here on.

Follow the fence to a stile and continue along the fence until the remnants of a stone wall are seen down the slope. Go down to be on the right of the wall. Go along until a stile is seen in the fence ahead. Cross it into a field. Keep to the right a of fence and head for tree a on a hillock. Go towards a white farmhouse and, when it can be seen, a derelict farm in the bottom right corner. Go through gates on to a tarmac track and go along it to a derelict cottage on the right. Go round the back of the cottage and cross a field to a ladder stile which can be seen crossing the fence ahead. Cross into a field go across it to a stile on right the of an occupied farmhouse. Cross on to Longshaw Lane and turn left along it to Ramshorn Road. Turn left along the road to a crossroads where the Old Blazing Star pub is available for refreshments. Turn left on to Beelow Lane and turn right on to a wide path, following it down. Go across a stile at the right corner into a field. Keep left and go downhill through two fields to reach a farm track. Cross the track to a stile and go over into a field. Veer over to the left to a gap in the hedge. Go through – still going downhill – and reach a stile at the bottom. Cross the stile on to road and turn left, downhill, into Oakamoor. Turn off left just before the river bridge on to a path and follow it to the car park.

REFRESHMENTS:
There are several pubs nearby.

Walk 22   LONGNOR AND HOLLINSCLOUGH $4^1/_4$m (7km)

Maps: OS Sheets Landranger 110; Outdoor Leisure 24.

A fairly easy walk with spectacular scenery.

Start: Longnor, cars may be parked in the square or on the main streets.

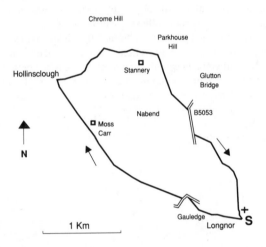

From the square, set off west over the crossroads. After passing the Horseshoe Inn, bear right along a minor road (not down the hill) and on approaching the farm at Gauledge, take the footpath left (as signposted). Continue, keeping the wall immediately on your right. Where the wall ends, head straight across the middle of the next field and over the stile on to a road. Turn left, walking downhill to Dunbrook and turning right after crossing the stream (signposted to Hollinsclough, $1^1/_4$ miles). In Hollinsclough, turn right at the road junction and after $^1/_4$ mile, take the track to the left just before a right hand bend. Cross over the cattle grid and follow the track towards **Chrome Hill**. After $^1/_4$ mile, take the right fork (signposted to Glutton Bridge). Cross the footbridge over the River Dove and on reaching the road at Stannery – close to **Parkhouse Hill**, turn right. Almost immediately, cross over the stile in the wall on the right and make for the right-angle of the wall to the left. Walk to the footbridge ahead and climb part way up Nabend Hill, veering left of the summit through a line of bushes towards the house at Near Nabend. Go over two stiles on the footpath, joining a track which leads to the B5053. Turn right on to the road up the hill, past a house at Highacres and, almost immediately afterwards, take the track left down the hill. Pass to the right of the second of two houses ahead and cross over the stile on the right, around which the ground may be boggy. Head up the hill immediately to the right of the house and on reaching another track, turn left, walking downhill again. At the entrance to the next farm, take the footpath right, up the hill, passing over the stile in the wall at the top. Longnor village can now be seen ahead. Continue on the footpath, keeping to the right of a wall and aiming slightly to the right of the church. At the junction with the road at Lanehead, turn left, cross Church Street and turn left down the main road (B5053). Shortly afterwards, turn left, back into the square at Longnor.

POINTS OF INTEREST:

Chrome and Parkhouse Hills – From the Hollinsclough road onwards, there are impressive views of these two spectacular limestone peaks.

There are extensive views of both the Manifold and Dove valleys on the walk.

REFRESHMENTS:

The Horseshoe Inn, Longnor (tel no: 0298 83262).
The Cheshire Cheese Hotel, Longnor (tel no: 0298 83218).
The Grapes Hotel, Market Place, Longnor (tel no: 0298 83494).
The Crewe & Harpur Arms Hotel, Longnor (tel no: 0298 83205).
The Manifold Restaurant, The Square, Longnor (tel no: 0298 83317).

Walk 23   TRAVELLERS REST AND THREE SHIRES HEAD   4¹/₂m (7km)

Maps: OS Sheets Landranger 119; Outdoor Leisure 24.

A pleasant all year round walk along ancient trails and through areas of Special Scientific Interest (SSI).

Start: At 032678; the Travellers Rest Inn.

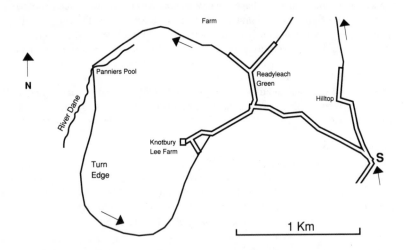

Walk towards Buxton for 500m, to just before the Derbyshire border. Go left at Quarnford Lodge along a minor road and after 100m turn right along another minor road. After 300m, just before a farm, go left over a stile by a gate and along an old green lane between gritstone walls. There are good views from here across Cheshire. Follow the made up track around left, past grouse butts, to a gate. Continue past the obvious clay pigeon shoot area and on to a farm. Go left in front of the farm and down through a swing gate. Keeping below the gritstone edge, cross the wall, left, through another swing gate and go across the front of the farm. Leave the farm along a track to another farm. Pass in front of this, and join a road to reach a T-junction. Turn right and follow the road along through a gate and continue to a right-hand bend then cut

54

down left along a wall for 100m to reach a road. Turn left through a gate and go down the valley past a rusty water spring to where a stream comes in from the **packhorse trail**. On arriving at the packhorse bridge at **Three Shires Head** turn left towards the River Dane.

Follow the track past Panniers Pool, an excellent summer swimming and picnic spot. Keep to the sandy track as it rises from the river and the valley bottom. Stay with the path past several farms. Most of the land to the left and right here was designated as an SSI in 1989. Eventually you reach a made-up road: continue along this, circling left to meet a stream. After 500m the road swings up and left, go right over a stile and follow the stream to meet the road again after about 200m. Follow the road up the hill keeping to the right until you regain the Travellers Rest.

POINTS OF INTEREST:
Packhorse Trail – Part of the ancient packhorse trail from the Cheshire plain to Buxton and the industrial Midlands.
Three Shires Head – The actual meeting point of Cheshire, Derbyshire, and Staffordshire. A meeting place for the 'flash' counterfeiters in days gone by with easy escapes into another county.

REFRESHMENTS:
The Travellers Rest, (tel no: 0298 24253).

Walk 24   ALTON AND BROOKLEYS LAKE $4^1/_2$m (7km)

Maps: OS Sheets Landranger 128; Pathfinder SK 04/14.

This is a good walk for the winter with one or two steep climbs to keep you warm and plenty of pubs in Alton.

Start: At 076424, Back Lane.

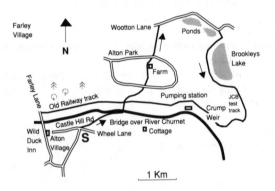

From Back Lane, with fields on the right, go to a farm at the junction with Castle Hill Road. Go through the farm gate to the right (but on the left of Wheel Lane). Go diagonally left across the large field to a stile about 200 yards away. Cross the stile on to a path down through trees to reach a farm track. Cross to the stile opposite and go through the field beyond to reach a bridge over the river. Cross to reach a path alone an old railway. Go over the stile opposite and then uphill, taking the middle of three paths, signed 'Public Footpath'. After going up some stone steps turn left for a few yards on a wide path. Ahead, on the right, is a stile over a high wire-mesh fence. Cross into Alton Park and head to the left of a farmhouse, then round it on to a tarmac track. Go right for a few yards to reach a flagstone path off to the left among trees. Take this path to a stile and cross into a field. Go directly across to a second stile and after crossing this go downhill to a squeezer stile in a stone wall. Go through and then across a farm track on to a worn path to reach, after a few yards, Wootton Lane.

Turn right on this road and go for about $^3/_4$ mile passing private Estate ponds and streams. Where the road turns sharp left, there is a small footpath sign and squeezer stile on the right. Go over and follow the path, and waymarks, which will guide you round Brookleys Lake on the JCB Test Track. At the end of the lake turn off the track over a waymarked stile. Go over a second stile and go along a bank on a worn path to reach a stile out on to a country road. Turn right and go along the left edge of the JCB establishment to a path at the end of it going uphill and on the left of a sandpit. Round the corner of the fence on the left and follow it down to an open gate. Go through and turn right, going diagonally down the bank on a worn path on to a tarmac track. Turn right and go through a gate and up the track to the Pumping Station at Crumpwood Weir. Pass the Pumping Station on the left and continue to a stile with the old canal on the right. Go over and continue on to the old railway path. Turn right along this back to the point it was crossed earlier in the walk and return back up the path to Alton. Alternatively carry on along the railway path to the bridge and then turn left up the road to Alton. This route has the advantage of a stop at the Wild Duck Inn halfway up the steep hill!

REFRESHMENTS:
Numerous in Alton.

57

Walk 25 RAKEWAY, FREEHAY AND WINNOTHDALE $4\frac{1}{2}$m (7km)

Maps: OS Sheets Landranger 119; Pathfinder SK 04/14.

A walk through fields and along country lanes.

Start: At 022419, in Rakeway Road about a mile south-east of
Cheadle.

Go north-west along Rakeway Road past the property called The Rakeway. Now go
left on a path that goes behind Plantation House, past the riding school and on to the
unclassified road between Mobberley and Winnothdale close to Mobberley Quarry.
Turn left along the road to Winnothdale. Bear right at a junction, then left at the next
on the lane towards Great Gate. Soon a footpath leads off to the left, going up past
Spring Farm. At the beginning of this footpath muddy conditions may be encountered
after heavy rain. Follow the path to a lane and turn left along it. At the T-junction
ahead is the Queen's Arms. Turn left at this T-junction, then go straight over the
crossroads at Freehay. The walk leaves the road by following the path to the right
about 300 yards further on. Towards the top of a rise the path goes to the right across
a field and then down through woodland to join Rakeway Road. Go left to the start.

REFRESHMENTS:
The Queen's Arms, (tel no: 0538 722383).

Walk 26   TITTESWORTH RESERVOIR   4¹/₂m (7km)

Maps: OS Sheets Landranger 118; Outdoor Leisure 24.
An interesting walk around the Severn Trent Reservoir.
Start: At 993603, the Visitor Centre.

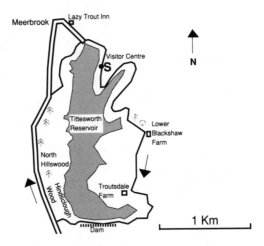

Walk south across the field and follow the well marked footpath round to the left to reach the **River Churnet**. Continue on to gain a cart track through the wood before turning off right and going down to cross a stream. The path rises to meet a cart track. Ahead take the right fork which brings you to the **reservoir** dam. Cross the dam and gain the woodland path which climbs steadily upwards until you are able to look down on to the ancient **Hindsclough Wood**. Turn right along the metalled road by drystone walls until you reach the car park and Fishery Office on the west side of the lake. There are superb views of the Western Gritstone Outcrops at this spot. Continue along the path to the causeway where the lake is divided by the roadway. Turn right and you will soon regain the car park entrance and the **Visitor Centre.** The small Northern lake is designated a conservation area and is not open to the general public. This whole lake area is rich in wildlife and you are advised to sit quietly somewhere and just enjoy what goes on around you.

POINTS OF INTEREST:
The River Churnet – The main feeder river for the reservoir which drains the Western Gritstone Edges.

Reservoir – The dam was constructed between 1959 and 1963 and provides water for the Potteries conurbation.

Hindsclough Wood – An ancient (medieval) wood of elm, ash, birch, oak, rowan and sycamore: At certain times it provides a safe haven for red deer.

Visitor Centre – Here you can learn about the rich flora and fauna of this area amongst which are red deer, badger, orchids and a profusion of water-based birds.

REFRESHMENTS:
A café is attached to the Visitor Centre and is open during the summer months.
The Lazy Trout, Meerbrook (tel no: 053 834 385).

Walk 27   **AROUND GRINDON**   4$\frac{1}{2}$m (7km)

Maps: OS Sheets Landranger 119; Outdoor Leisure 24.

A fairly easy walk with interesting limestone hill and valley scenery.

Start: At 095561, Wettonmill, where there is off the road parking on the valley road to the west of the bridge.

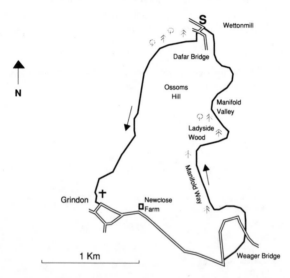

After parking, turn left along the road and then right at the crossroads (signposted to Butterton, 1$\frac{1}{4}$ miles). Refreshments are available at the shop just over the bridge. Bear right on the road (avoiding the ford) and cross the footbridge immediately on the left, on to **Ossoms Hill**. Follow the path up the hill for a short distance until it forks. Take the right fork, keeping the fence on the right. Approximately 70 yards further on, cross a stile over a fence, which is obscured behind a tree and easily missed. The path beyond climbs upwards, but where it dies out, continue at approximately the same height, following the bend of the Hoo Brook below and keeping above the wood on the right. After bending round the hill a stile is reached. Cross and walk straight across the field ahead, aiming for a stile slightly to the left of a gate. Bear right to join the track leading from the farm on the right. Follow the track past the church on the left and to the outskirts of Grindon. At the road junction just past the church, turn left and then immediately right. As the road forks, bear left and then left again on to the road leading to Wetton. Continue along the road, taking a steep, sharp left-hand bend and branching right on to a path immediately afterwards. Proceed rapidly downhill on the path, crossing a stile in a group of trees at the bottom, on to the Manifold Way track. Turn left along the track, cross the Grindon-Wetton road and follow the track past **Thor's Cave** (above right, in the hillside). The bed of the River Manifold on the right is usually dry in dry weather. On reaching a crossroads, continue straight on, to the Wettonmill crossroads. Again carry straight on, back to the parking places on the right.

POINTS OF INTEREST:

Ossoms Hill – There are good views across the Manifold Valley to Ecton Hill and Wetton Hill from a short way up the slope of Ossoms Hill. From the western side of the hill, there are extensive views north-westwards to Butterton and the moors beyond.

Thor's Cave – A natural limestone cave in a cliff which rises over 300 feet from the bed of the River Manifold and which is accessible by a path over a footbridge. There is evidence of human habitation from 10,000 BC until Roman times.

REFRESHMENTS:

The shop, Wettonmill

The Cavalier Inn, Grindon (tel no: 053 88 285).

Walk 28   **HIGH PEAK TRAIL**   4¹/₂m (7km)

Maps: OS Sheets Landranger 119; Outdoor Leisure 24.

An easy walk, half on a disused railway track, now the High Peak Trail, the other half along old lanes.

Start: At 194582, the Minninglow car park.

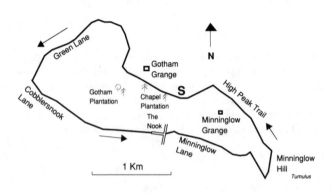

From the car park take the High Peak Trail, crossing the road that goes to Pikehall. Follow the Trail as it goes through a wood, Chapel Plantation, and heads for Gotham and the notable Gotham Bend. Continue on the Trail for another ¹/₂ mile or so beyond the bend to where a lane crosses it. This is Green Lane: turn left down it and in less than a mile you come to a junction of two old ways. Go left along Cobblersnook Lane.

After about ¹/₂ mile the wall on your left disappears: keep with a wall on the right across a field and pick up the lane again at the far side. About ¹/₂ mile further on you come to The Nook and the lane becomes metalled. Soon after the cottage you cross a minor road and continue in the same direction along Minninglow Lane.

A mile further on, by a pond on your right, the lane curves left for a few yards, then bends sharply right to meet the High Peak Trail again. Turn left along the Trail for a pleasant level walk of about a mile back to the car park.

POINTS OF INTEREST:
The High Peak Trail – The old railway was an industrial line carrying lime products. Look over the sides now and then to consider the work entailed in building this line. The lanes on the walk were part of an old packhorse way from Hartington to Wirksworth.

REFRESHMENTS:
No refreshments are available on the walk but it's only a short trip to Newhaven and the hotel there, or to Elton.

Walk 29   DILHORNE AND TICKHILL LANE   4¹/₂m (7km)

Maps: OS Sheets Landranger 118; Pathfinder SJ 84/94.

An easy walk across fields, through woodland and along a country lane.

Start: At 971435, the recreation centre in Dilhorne.

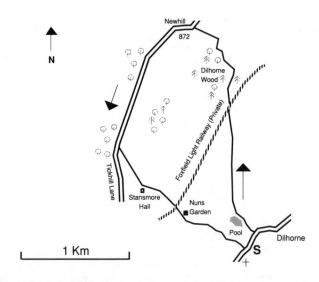

Turn right along the road and, after about 100 yards, a stile leads to a track past a pool. Just after the pool go into the field on your right. The path crosses the fields (using stiles) towards woodland. Pass through the wood and cross over the private **Foxfield Railway** (beware of steam trains) into the woodland at the other side. Through this section of woodland the path is rather indistinct, but can be followed as it curves right and then left to fields. Proceed up the fields to a track between stone walls. Bear left towards New Hill Farm. Beyond the farm the walk reaches Tickhill Lane. Turn left along it for nearly a mile until a stile on the left leads across fields towards Stansmore Hall Farm.

Before the farm is reached the path emerges from the fields on to a section of the farm driveway. On reaching the farm itself do not enter the yard, but go across the field with the farm on your right. Having left the farm behind, continue along the field with the hedge on your right for a short distance, then go straight ahead and down to cross the railway again. Very shortly the path crosses an old bridge over a small stream. On the left side of the path near the bridge is a small square area of raised ground and local tradition maintains that this is the Nun's Garden. Possibly it had connections with Caverswall Castle which is just over a mile away.

The route now goes up the field ahead, over a stile and turns to the left. You now have a fence on your left for a few yards. Cross straight over the field to find the next stile, and then continue straight ahead to return to Dilhorne.

POINTS OF INTEREST:

The Foxfield Light Railway – The private railway which is crossed twice on this walk was originally the line which transported coal from the Foxfield Colliery in Dilhorne. The colliery ceased working during the 1960's.

REFRESHMENTS:

The Royal Oak, Dilhorne (tel no: 0782 392774).
Charlie Bassets, Dilhorne (tel no: 0782 392115).

Walk 30   **WRINEHILL AND MADELEY**   4¹/₂m (7km)
Maps: OS Sheets Landranger 118; Pathfinder SJ 64/74.
A well-marked route visiting the attractive village of Madeley.
Start: At 753468, on the Wrinehill to Checkley/Bridgemere road
just before the railway bridge.

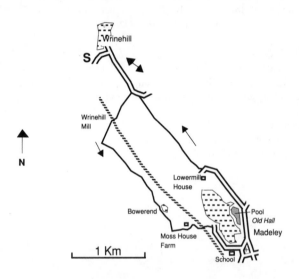

Walk to Wrinehill and at the Blue Bell turn right for 500m until the road bears left.
Turn right down a lane to Wrinehill Mill. Go under the railway and follow the lane
down left past **Wrinehill Hall** to the farm and a crossing of the River Lea. Immediately
after crossing the river turn left over a small stream and stile to follow the river
upstream. Go over a stile and diagonally right to a bare hilltop. Follow the remains of
a hedgerow over another stile and keep straight ahead and follow the edge of the
wood over two further stiles. Go diagonally right. Follow the farm drive to a cattle
grid and turn left down the hill past Moss House Farm. Go over the railway then first
right round the estate, in Madeley, and turn left towards the church and the Sir John
Offley School (see Note to Walk 46). Go left behind the church and over the stream.
Go first left and continue towards the village centre past **Madeley Old Hall**, **Madeley**

68

Pool, the Offley Arms, and the Bridge Inn. Just past the Bridge Inn turn left down Furnace Lane to Lowermill House. After 500m, by a left-hand bend, go straight ahead following a footpath sign. Take the hedge past a hollow and keep straight on to a field corner. Go over the stile here and follow the hedge: there are fine views across Cheshire. Keep ahead to a stile by a pond, then go diagonally left towards the houses. At the main road walk 500m to the Blue Bell and turn left to the start point.

POINTS OF INTEREST:
Wrinehill Hall – Actually Wrinehill Hall Farm built on the site of Wrinehill Hall the old family hall of the Hawkestone and Egerton families.
Madeley Old Hall – A well preserved Jacobean building of 1647 with a cheeky inscription on its front. You can stay Bed and Breakfast here.
Madeley Pool – There are plans to turn this into a wildlife haven and conservation area.

REFRESHMENTS:
The Blue Bell, Wrinehill (tel no: 0270 820425).
The Offley Arms, Madeley (tel no: 0782 750242).
The Bridge Inn, Madeley (tel no: 0782 750977).

Walk 31   ILAM, MUSDEN AND BLORE   4¹/₂m (7km)

Maps: OS Sheets Landranger 119; Outdoor Leisure 24.

A fairly easy walk over variable and occasionally muddy ground in wet weather.

Start: The village of Ilam.

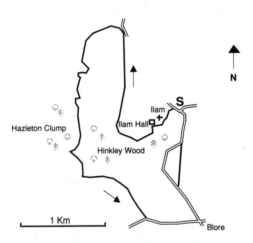

Find the monument immediately to the north of the bridge over the River Manifold where cars may be parked at the side of the road. From the monument, head north-west away from the river, passing several ornate cottages on the right. At a junction shortly afterwards, take the left fork (to Ilam Hall), but then fork immediately left again (to Dovedale House). After a few yards, turn left through a gate and follow the path first to **Ilam Church**, then through a kissing gate (keeping the church on the left) to **Ilam Hall.** (Refreshments can be taken at the Manor Tea Rooms to the rear of the hall.) On approaching the hall, turn left and walk down a flight of steps to the River Manifold and then bear right, following a path (called Paradise Walk) along its bank. Shortly afterwards, pass the **Ilam Boil Holes** and the **Battle Stone** on the right, with **Hinkley Wood** up on the left. Continue through two stiles (there are pleasant views of the river from the footbridge immediately after the first of these) and on until the River Lodge is approached. Theoretically, a one penny toll should be paid to pass through the garden and on to the road. At the road, turn left and follow it over the bridge at Rushley (where the bed of the Manifold is usually dry in dry weather). At a sharp right-hand bend shortly afterwards, take the track left (signposted to Musden Low and Calton Moor) through the farmyard and, after a short distance follow it round a sharp right-hand bend. About 100 yards after this, as the track climbs and veers left, look out for, and take, an easily-missed sunken, grassed-over track to the left. This climbs fairly steeply, first arcing to the right, then bending to the left past a signpost to Ilam and Rushley. Continue straight ahead until the track peters out, then carry on past a hummock on the left, keeping a wall on the right. Cross a stile by a gate ahead and then follow the path in a right-hand arc to Musden Grange. Take the path left, out from Musden Grange and then, bearing left, aim for a green path on the opposite hillside to the left of Hazelton Clump. Head down the slope, cross the remains of two walls and a depression and then climb on to the aforementioned path. Pass through two gates and continue to a road. Turn left on this, then, at the crossroads, turn left again to Ilam, following the road until it passes a parking and picnic site on the right. Shortly after this, take a path to the right, down the hillside, to rejoin the road at the bottom. Then walk over the Manifold bridge and back to the monument.

POINTS OF INTEREST:
Ilam Church – This contains the tomb of St Bertram, a Mercian prince who became a hermit after his wife and child were devoured by wolves. The Saxon font depicts carved scenes from his life and in the graveyard there are two carved Saxon crosses.
Ilam Hall – The current hall was built in 1840 and houses a youth hostel, a National Trust shop, a tea shop (open in the summer). There are magnificent trees in the grounds.
The Ilam Boil Holes – The waters of the River Manifold, having gone underground at Wettonmill, reappear through the boil holes just before the weir. Slightly upstream, before the footbridge, the waters of the River Hamps reappear through the Hamps Spring, on the far bank of the Manifold, and run into the bed of the latter.
The Battle Stone – This is thought to be of mid-eleventh century origin and is associated with the struggle between the Saxons and the Danes.
Hinkley Wood – This is being replanted owing to Dutch Elm disease, but is still beautifully coloured in October.

REFRESHMENTS:
The Manor Tea Rooms, Ilam Hall, Ilam (tel no: 033 529 245).
The Izaak Walton Hotel, Ilam (tel no: 033 529 555/275).

Walk 32   FLASH AND GRADBACH   5m (8km)

Maps: OS Sheets Landranger 119; Outdoor Leisure 24.

An attractive walk over seldom visited territory. Fine views and good picnic spots.

Start: At 025672, in Flash.

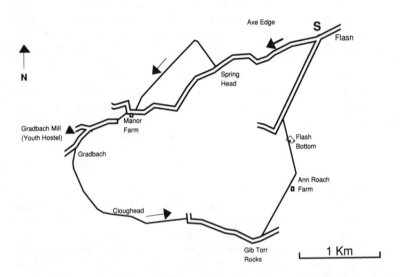

Leave from the front of the New Inn and head westwards past the square Wesleyan Chapel (1784/1821). Continue for about 1km downhill, with good views of **Axe Edge** to your right, to Spring Head Farm. At the farm buildings either side of the road turn right at a footpath sign and descend to a stile and footbridge over a small stream. Cross these and follow the track uphill to where it begins to flatten out. There is an obvious stile on the right at this point. Go left (south), however, and follow the broad ridge down over stiles and through gates, keeping to the left of the gritstone walls, until it is possible to exit on to the minor road by Manor Farm. Turn right here for 50m, then go left through a gate/stile and follow the stream left to a footbridge and another lane. Turn right along this lane for 500m, taking the left fork (**Gradbach Mill** and Youth Hostel are down to the right at this point).

Just past the Scout HQ turn left up a gated lane past a farmhouse and continue straight on to contour the hillside leftwards following a sometimes indistinct track. It can be boggy here. The track eventually becomes a footpath which leads to Cloughhead and a road junction. Go straight ahead (eastwards) past two road junctions to Gib Torr outcrops and the beginnings of a forested area. Where the road levels out turn left for the signposted Ann Roach Farm, and keep to the right (east) side of the escarpment across the moor. Go behind Ann Roach Farm and follow the trackway by the gritstone wall to contour down to Flash Bottom Farm. Care is needed here to keep your feet dry. Exit leftwards past the farm and cross the farm lane to a stile. Go over and diagonally left across the next field towards a house and a set of steps that lead up to the minor road. Turn right along this road to return to the village of **Flash**.

POINTS OF INTEREST:

Axe Edge – Forms the watershed between the Irish Sea (River Dane) and the North Sea (Rivers Dove and Manifold into the Trent).

Gradbach Mill – A water-powered spinning mill of 18th-century origin now converted to a youth hostel (1980/81). The spot still evokes early industrial organization and times.

Flash – At 1518 feet above sea level the highest village in England. It gave its name to the slang term for counterfeit money as in past days 'coiners' had their headquarters here.

REFRESHMENTS:
The New Inn, Flash (tel no: 0298 22941).

Walk 33   **HULME END, WETTONMILL AND ECTON**   5m (8km)
Maps: OS Sheets Landranger 119; Outdoor Leisure 24.
A fairly easy walk with interesting limestone valley and hill scenery.
Start: At 102594, the Hulme End car park.

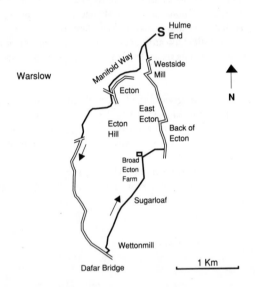

Turn right down the Manifold Way track, and enter an incised gorge. Continue along the track, crossing straight over the minor road from Warslow, after which the former **Ecton Copper Mine** workings appear on the left. Cross the footbridge over the Warslow Brook and on meeting the road, carry on straight ahead through the (former railway) tunnel, but beware of the traffic! Then continue along the road (for approximately $1\frac{1}{4}$ miles) to Wettonmill. At the road junction at Wettonmill, turn left over the bridge. (Refreshments can be taken at the shop on the right.) From the bridge, take the road left and at the junction shortly afterwards, follow the path straight on (signposted to Back of Ecton, $1\frac{1}{4}$ miles), proceeding through a farmyard. Carry on up the dry valley ahead, towards **Sugarloaf**, a limestone outcrop at its head. Walk to the foot of Sugarloaf, then follow the steep path on its left-hand side. At the top of the slope, cross the stile ahead and go immediately left over a second stile (which is easily missed). Continue on the path, keeping first a fence and then a wall, on the right. At the end of the field, carry on with the wall on the left. Go over a stile and on to a junction with a track. Turn left along the track and just before a farmhouse, fork right through a broken-down wall. Bear left over a stile and turn right through a gate. Continue up the field ahead, keeping the wall on your right, to cross a stile near the top of the incline. From the top, walk straight down the steep slope towards the house ahead, keeping the wall to the left. At the bottom, turn left on to the road and pass through Back of Ecton to a road junction in the Manifold Valley. Turn right, but at Westside Mill shortly afterwards, turn left on to a footpath and footbridge over the river. The path then veers right away from the river and crosses a stile in the fence ahead. Follow the path through the next field, which can be wet underfoot, heading towards the Manifold Way track. Cross on to the track by way of a stile, turn right and the Hulme End car park is just ahead.

POINTS OF INTEREST:

Ecton Copper Mines – These were once the deepest mines in Britain and, at 1400 feet, one of the deepest in Europe. The mine produced almost a million tons of the mineral (worth £300.000) but have been unworked since 1890.

Sugarloaf – An unusual, steep and impressive limestone outcrop, with good views from its summit across the Manifold Valley to Ossoms Hill.

REFRESHMENTS:

The Manifold Valley Hotel, Hulme End (tel no: 0298 84537).
The Shop, Wettonmill.

Walk 34   ROACH END AND DANEBRIDGE   5m (8km)

Maps: OS Sheets Landranger 118; Outdoor Leisure 24.

A relatively dry walk visiting some surprisingly pretty countryside. The last part can feel exposed in windy or cold conditions.

Start: At 996645, Roach End.

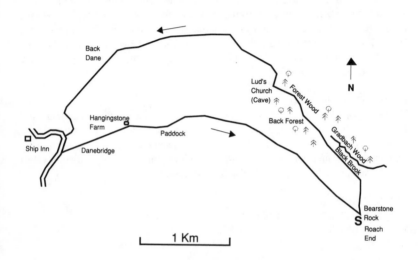

Go down the lane on your right for a few metres then over a stile on your left to follow the wall down rightwards to the wood edge. Turn left and take the track that follows the edge for about 1km until you arrive at the entrance to Lud's Church (see Note to Walk 94). Go down through this and exit the other end. Descend the hillside rightwards to meet a path going left that follows Black Brook but about 50m above the Brook. Follow this path for about 1km to where it breaks out into open grassland with good views. Follow the well-marked path over stiles and across fields past Back Dane Farm to enter woodland again. Continue through this woodland for about 500m to meet the River Dane near Danebridge. The Ship Inn is approximately 300m up the hill to your right at this point.

At Danebridge turn left for 100m, then left again at a footpath signed for Back Forest and Gradbach. Go up the narrow snicket going north-east through a small wood. Exit over a stile and head for Hangingstone Farm. The **Hangingstone** is the jutting-out gritstone outcrop on the escarpment. Follow the track past the farm to reach Paddock Farm. Keep to the track below the ridge, gradually gaining altitude. The track passes the Back Forest crags, and eventually arrives at Roach End and the start.

POINTS OF INTEREST:
The Hangingstone – Two plaques used to be fixed to this buttress; one commemorated the death of a faithful dog, and the other, a member of the Brocklehurst family.

REFRESHMENTS:
The Ship Inn, Wincle (tel no: 0260 227217).

Walk 35   **BREWOOD AND CHILLINGTON**   5m (8km)

Maps: OS Sheets Landranger 127; Pathfinder SJ 80/90.

A fine example of Staffordshire parkland.

Start: At 883086, the centre of Brewood.

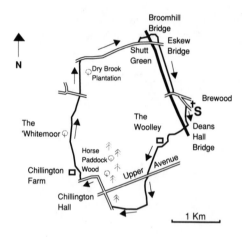

Head south along Church Road, past the Parish Church, and bear left at the bottom –
a public alleyway is seen on the right. Take this between houses to an unsurfaced road
where a left turn and an immediate right at a footpath sign take you across fields to
emerge at Deans Hall Bridge. Turn right across the canal bridge and follow the unmade
road to The Woolley. At the farm continue follow the Staffordshire Way sign to a
bend with a pool on the right and a stile on the left. Cross the stile and the following
the field to Upper Avenue, the drive leading to Chillington Hall. Cross 'The Avenue',
with the Hall in the distance to the right and, still following the Staffordshire Way
signs, cross another field to arrive at a green lane. Go right as far as a small, white,
thatched cottage where the track became more of an estate road. Continue to reach a
minor surfaced road. Turn right along this road to the entrance gates of **Chillington
Hall**.

Continue along the edge of Horse Paddock Wood where the road bears left and, at the drive to Chillington Farm, turn right. Pass the farmhouse and farm buildings on your left and walk between two outbuildings ahead into a field. Keep the hedge on your left until it turns 90° left where you continue ahead to a gate on the right-hand edge of a stand of trees. Climb the stile at the side and continue to another gate and a cross track. Going right, pass a house on the left and a small pool on the right. In the field turn left to follow the garden hedge for about 60 yards to its first corner where a crop-free path leads directly ahead across a field to a gap in the opposite hedge. Through the gap the now distinct path bears right and over a wooden bridge. Go up the left-hand side of the next field arriving at the opening into a green lane which brings you on to the road at Oakley.

Turn right along the road and then quickly left at the drive to Oakley Farm to come to a right-hand bend. The route is straight ahead on a clear track until it, too, turns sharp right. Still continuing straight ahead the route is not apparent, so line up on a neatly shaped oak tree in the distance and walk roughly parallel to Dry Brook Plantation. Continue to a hedge gap on to a narrow lane. Ahead lies the expanse of **Belvide Reservoir.**

Turn right along the lane for about $^3/_4$ mile to Lee Fields Farm on the right. Shortly after the farm there is a public footpath post on the left. Follow this to an abandoned cottage. Pass in front of the cottage and follow a distinct path to arrive at Broomhill Bridge (Bridge 16) over the Shropshire Union Canal. Turn right along the towpath and follow it all the way to Brewood Bridge (Bridge 14). Climb to the road into **Brewood**.

POINTS OF INTEREST:

Chillington – Mentioned in the Domesday Book and passed in marriage to the Giffard family in the 12th century, thus beginning an unbroken association of 800 years. The Parkland owes much of its present form to the work of Capability Brown. The Hall is open to the public on Thursday afternoons from May to August/September and on certain Sundays and Bank Holidays.

Belvide Reservoir – A canal feeder and now a nature reserve being developed by the Royal Society for the Protection of Birds.

Brewood – A delightful Staffordshire village with a long history. Originally a Roman Fort defending the nearby Watling Street.

REFRESHMENTS:

Many pubs and services in Brewood.

Walk 36   CIRCUIT OF RUDYARD LAKE   5m (8km)

Maps: OS Sheets Landranger 118; Outdoor Leisure 24.

A walk for all seasons, around the Victorian resort of Rudyard.
Start: At 955579, the site of the former Rudyard Station on the
B5331 just outside Rudyard.

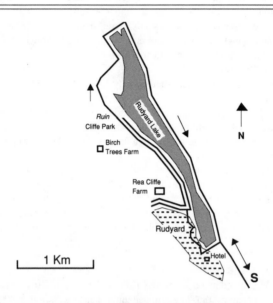

Walk north along the track of the old railway or, as a non-walking alternative – and
only if it is running – take the miniature railway service as far as the Dam on **Rudyard
Lake**. At the dam cross the footbridge, left, over the overflow on to the dam itself.
There are fine views along the lake. Cross the dam, and go up the slope and through a
gate to reach Lake Road. The Hotel Rudyard is on your left at this point. Turn right
along Lake Road and take the track which bears left past the back of the houses. As
you approach the caravan site go left up the hill. The track narrows: where it levels
out go right to join another path and descend with this for a short way. Just before the
house at the bottom of the slope turn left. You enter woodland, and after a few hundred
metres the rising track forks with a small path going off and down to the right. Follow
this down over an open area to reach a wide lane, (Reacliffe Road). Turn right and

after a short way turn left to pass along the backs of the lakeside properties. Follow the lane past the Sailing Club and the large house of **Cliffe Park**.

Continue on and down and cross a stile by a gate. Beyond, after 200m, you turn right at the head of the lake. A large reedy area is to your right and you cross an obviously man-made **Cut**. At the bridge by the parking area turn right along the track of the former railway for about 4km to reach the site of the old Rudyard Station and the car park.

POINTS OF INTEREST:

Rudyard Lake – Created in 1831 to feed the Trent and Mersey Canal system and still in use for this purpose. The lake can sometimes look like the estuary of a small Cornish resort. On the dam, note the masons's marks used to calculate payments due to craftsmen.

Cliffe Park – Originally a home for one of the directors of the North Staffordshire Railway Company, then a Youth Hostel, but now a private home, again.

The Cut – Brings water from the River Dane, which flows into the Irish Sea, to Rudyard Lake which flows, via canals, into the North Sea. The Cut is so nearly level that the water sometimes flows back the opposite way!

REFRESHMENTS:

The Hotel Rudyard, Rudyard (tel no: 053833 208).
The Poachers Tavern, (tel no: 053833 294).
The Poachers Tavern is some 200m west of the car park towards Rudyard village.
Refreshments are also sometimes available in the car park.

Walk 37   **WROTTESLEY PARK**   5m (8km)

Maps: OS Sheets Landranger 138 & 139; Pathfinder SJ 80/90.

A gentle walk through attractive rolling countryside.

Start: At 856021, the lay by on the A41, near the entrance to Wrottesley Golf Club.

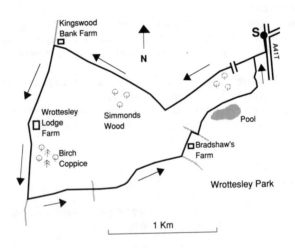

Cross the road and walk north along the pavement as far as the public footpath steps opposite Shop Lane. Go over the stile and turn left to follow the hedge and then a wall to the field corner where a right turn brings you to a three-way path sign. Follow the one indicating path number 02A, going straight ahead to the corner and a stile into a garden. Pass through the garden to the left of the pool and emerge through a wooden gate. Go straight ahead on the wide track in front as far as a Y-junction.

Take the right-hand fork towards a white shed and turn right to follow the edge of Simmonds Wood. Where the track goes right, walk straight ahead through a hunter's gate and then on and through another gate into a green lane to pass the Coach House and arrive at the track junction by Kingswood Bank Farm. Turn left in front of the semi-detached houses and continue along the farm track to Wrottesley Lodge Farm.

There are good views to the right. Go through the farm and head for the edge of Birch Coppice and from there towards another stand of trees. Before reaching the trees turn left, by an electricity pole keeping a hedge on your left.

Follow the track for a mile to Bradshaws Farm. Pass to the left of the houses ahead, with three diesel pumps on your right, to reach a tarmac track. Turn right, and then left along the edge of some trees. Soon this track swings right to emerge at a large pool – with a host of waterfowl – on the right and the converted apartments of **Wrottesley Hall** on the left.

Follow the track past the Hall, with the iron fence separating you from the Hall drive, and continue to a left bend which you follow to join the Staffordshire Way. Soon climb a stile on the left and turn right along the drive to reach the golf course. To the left is the Club House and a Staffordshire Way sign. Follow it through woodland, over a sleeper bridge, and on to the path you walked earlier. Turn right and retrace your steps to the lay by.

POINTS OF INTEREST:

Wrottesley Hall – Formerly the home of the Wrottesley family, the manor itself pre-dates the Norman Conquest. The old Hall was totally destroyed by fire towards the end of the last century, along with some priceless literary treasures. The present house dates from the early 1920's.

Walk 38 OKEOVER, BLORE AND COLDWALL BRIDGE 5m (8km)

Maps: OS Sheets Landranger 119; Pathfinder SK 04/14.

A steady ascent through Okeover Park to the hamlet of Blore with fine views towards Dove Dale.

Start: At 164482, the car park near Okeover Bridge.

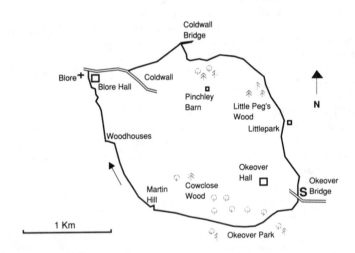

Ahead and to the right is a shallow tree lined valley ascending the hill. Take a line (no clear path) roughly along the lower right-hand trees to the top of the hill where, to the right, stands a derelict house. Go straight ahead to the gap in the wood, cross the stile, go along the wood and aim for the single stone gate post seen ahead and slightly left. At the post go left and cross the stile ahead on to a walled track leading to a farm. Near the track end turn sharply right across a broken wall, pass the farm house to the left and reach a path along the field boundary. Follow the path across three fields to join a walled track to Woodhouses Farm. Go through the gate, pass the farm buildings and reach a narrow lane that leads to Blore with its 14th-century small church and 16th-century hall (now a holiday camp site). Continue to a cross-roads. The road going left to right is the early 18th-century turnpike from Cheadle (Staffordshire) to

Thorpe (Derbyshire). Turn right and follow the road to Coldwall Farm. Turn left, still on the turnpike route, down the farm drive to a rough track beyond, and enter a field via a gate. There are superb views from here of the limestone reef hills, Bunster (left) and Thorpe Cloud (right), at the entrance to Dove Dale.

The footpath descends steeply on a direct line on to Coldwall Bridge (built 1726) whereas the turnpike took a less direct and less steep route. Beyond the bridge a surfaced path passes a milestone inscribed Cheadle 11 miles – measured to the Danish settlement of Thorpe at the top of the hill. Go through a small wood beyond the bridge and stile, and continue downstream again on a clear path through a small wood beyond which the path swings away from the river to reach a second small wood. There a waymarker points the way over a stile to the far side. Keep straight ahead up the small slope. – take a line just right of the dead tree to reach a track adjacent to a farm, after crossing a wooden stile. Turn right along the track for 100 yards, then go left to cross a stile and field to a stile in the left corner. Cross the next field in a similar fashion, arriving at the river again by an attractive weir. From here the path goes straight across the field to the old mill building and the road where the walk started.

REFRESHMENTS:
The Okeover Arms, Mapleton (tel no: 033529 305).

Walk 39   RUSHTON SPENCER AND GUN END   5m (8km)

Maps: OS Sheets Landranger 119; Outdoor Leisure 24.

A varied walk, sometimes wet, through remote parts of North Staffordshire.

Start: At 936624, the Staffordshire County council car park in the old railway yard at Rushton Spencer.

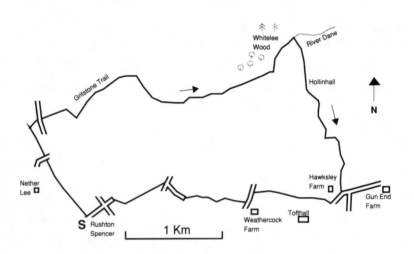

Leave the car park past the Knot Inn and pass the renovated station of the old North Staffordshire Railway Company (The Knotty). Follow the Staffordshire Way markings north along the old permanent way for 1km. About 300m after crossing a small lane follow the Staffordshire Way sign down the embankment left, by a bridge, and then turn right to follow the Gritstone Trail under the bridge. Cross the road and head directly across fields, with a sharp right, over the first stile to meet the Cut (see Note to Walk 36). Turn left and stroll along the Cut for about 2km to a weir and footbridge at Whitelee. (The Gritstone Trail goes left after a further 1km along the Cut, but you keep straight on.) At the footbridge at Whitelee go right over a stile, over the Cut, up and through a squeezer and head up the steep bank to Hollenhall Farm. Go to the left of the farm barns and right of the house. Turn left in front of the farmhouse and follow the lane towards Gun End main road. There is a café (Gun End Farm) 200m left at this junction, but our route actually goes right 100m before the junction is reached, along an old lane past the front of Hawksley Farm. Continue for about 1km: Toft Hall is on your left, and there are fine views to Heaton and the Cheshire plain. At a lane turn left for 100m then right, just before a junction, over a stile. Follow the boundary to the bottom left of the field, then go left through two squeezers and continue direct to a stile ahead. Go over the stile and head across and down to a squeezer. Beyond this go over a stile to a farm lane. After 100m, at a junction by another farm, cross the road and go immediate left over two stiles. Continue diagonally right, staying to the right of a stream and high up on the bank, to cross some well-made stiles. Descend to a footbridge. Cross this to reach a farm and pass the farmhouse through a gate. Go down the lane to the Cut and right along this over a stile to a bridge. Turn left at the bridge and down the lane to cross the main road and finish back at the Knot Inn.

REFRESHMENTS:
The Knot Inn, Rushton Spencer (tel no: 0260 226238).
The Gun End Farm Cafe.

Walk 40   HAUGHTON AND BERRY RING   5m (8km)

Maps: OS Sheets Landranger 127; Pathfinder SJ 82/92.

A fine walk through pleasant agricultural land.

Start: At 862214, the car park by the bridge in Station Road, Haughton.

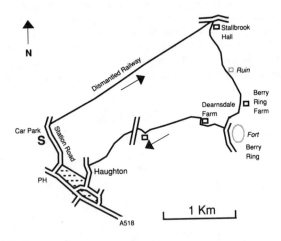

From the car park go right, under the bridge, and follow the old Wellington/Stafford railway bed for $1^{1}/_{2}$ miles to a minor lane and what used to be a level crossing. Here go right, and immediately right again, through a gate to follow the track to the right of Stallbrook Hall Farm. Arriving at a field edge you will see, to your left, a solitary oak tree which has been waymarked with yellow paint. Make your way to this and then head across the field to a hunter's gate in the opposite hedge, keeping to the left of another waymarked oak. In the next field continue ahead to the corner of a derelict farm and then follow two oak trees to another hunter's gate. Ahead is Berry Ring and, to your left, Stafford Castle.

Following the line of the yellow arrow, cross the next field to a metal gate in the hedge and so join the farm road up to the tarmac around **Berry Ring**. Shortly you reach the drive to Dearnsdale Farm on your right: follow this down to the opposite gate – to the left of the farmhouse. Go through and follow the track to the right, between two barns, and then left along the hedged and fenced track.

Passing a pool on the left, go through the gate at the end of the track and turn left for a few yards to, and through, a double gate. This takes you over a stream: go right to follow the opposite bank to the field corner. Here go left for a few yards to where, on the right, there is a fence stile. Go over this, passing between the house and the garage, and cross the drive to a gate into a field. In the field go left with the hedge to emerge at a lane where a left turn for 20 yards will bring you to a fence stile on the right.

Cross the stile and head across the field towards a gate. To the left of the gate, and recessed, is a small stile and footbridge. Go over and walk diagonally left across the next field to a corner stile into the Severn Trent service track. Follow the track to a lane and turn left to a public footpath sign on the right, immediately before the 30 mph signs. Go right over the fence stile and along the footpath, continually following the edge of the housing estate, to Station Road. Turn right along the road to arrive back at the Car Park.

POINTS OF INTEREST:

Berry Ring – An ancient defensive hill fort on a natural hillock. The hill top is at 450 feet.

Walk 41 MILLDALE, STANSHOPE AND ALSTONEFIELD 5m (8km)

Maps: OS Sheets Landranger 119; Outdoor Leisure 24.

A walk with beautiful views of Dove Dale from the lesser- used Staffordshire bank.

Start: At 135548, the public car park, Hope Dale.

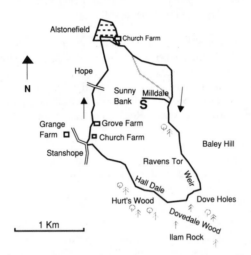

Walk down from the car park into **Milldale** where there is a delightful packhorse bridge and information barn. Between the Gents toilet and Mill Cottage is a narrow twisting path rising steeply for approximately 30 yards before turning left along the hillside. The path is clear and well stiled, ascending in the early stages to give fine views down into Dove Dale before descending to continue along the river's edge, where, on a quiet day, you may see a dipper or two. Follow the riverside path and shortly after passing Dove Holes (caves) a wall is reached with a slit stile. *Ignore it,* turning right along the clear path up Hall Dale. Cross the stile at the top into a field where the path veers right to cross two more stiles on to a rough track by a footpath sign. Turn left to reach a road, then right on the track between Stanshope Hall and the farm. This is part of the packhorse way from Ilam to Alstonefield. It descends to the road in Hope Dale, and via a stile opposite, continues steeply up the hillside, swinging left at the top to follow the boundary wall to a stile and gate. Over the stile keep straight ahead turning right at the road and immediately right again to reach **Alstonefield** village green and its 16th-century coaching inn, *The George*. Continue past the green, turning right at the end to pass the Manor House (1587) and church, beyond which the road narrows to the packhorse way known as Millway Lane. The lane descends to the riverside in Milldale where the walk effectively started.

N.B. An alternative finish is via a clear field path from a footpath sign near the church. The final section is very steep and can be hazardous if the walker is not properly shod, but does have the advantage of unimpeded views.

POINTS OF INTEREST

Milldale – The packhorse bridge, known as Viator's Bridge, is referred to in 1676 edition of Izaak Walton's *Compleat Angler*.

Alstonefield – Originally a Saxon settlement. Once a busy market town – its charter was granted in 1308 – and the crossroads of several packhorse ways. The church is the third on the same site. It has a Norman South doorway and chancel arch and fine 17th-century pews.

REFRESHMENTS:

The George, Alstonefield (tel no: 033527 205).
Shop and Tea Rooms, Alstonefield.

Walk 42   SIX LANE ENDS AND TURNER'S POOL   5m (8km)
Maps: OS Sheets Landranger 118; Outdoor Leisure 24.
A reasonable, all year round walk with unusual views of the Roaches Estate.
Start: At 963618, Six Lane Ends.

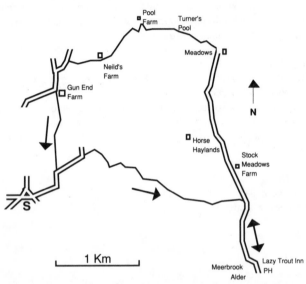

Go east along the lane past the old spoil heaps, now reclaimed, and head for the crest of the ridge. From hereon there are constant and changing views of the **Roaches Estate**. Continue down the lane and at a wood turn left towards the farm. At the left bend just before the farm, head straight down over a field to an awkward stile with a fingerpost. Continue in the direction indicated to cross a small stream on the right near a farm. Turn diagonally left and go past two ash trees to a stile and footbridge. At the lane go left to meet a road. At this point a detour right for 750m brings you to the Lazy Trout pub at Meerbrook. Alternately turn left and follow the public footpath along the private farm road for 1.5kms to reach Meadow Farm. Note the barn inscription at Stock Meadow Farm, to the right on the way.

    At Meadow Farm go left over two stiles and then left along the farm lane for

92

about 250m, keeping to the right of the fence, to cross a stile and small stream. Head straight across the next field to cross the stream beside a right-angled fence. Go diagonally left to a stile by a wood edge and follow this edge over two more stiles to reach the north side of Turner's Pool, a pleasant picnic spot.

Go past the Pool along the lane for 100m and turn left before the stream by the farm and paddock. Go over a bridge and stile, and head up diagonally right to a gate. Go through and turn left along the field boundary. Go through another gate and make for a stile ahead. Go over this and on to another gate by some holly trees. Continue along the indistinct lane and pass the farm on its left to reach the farm lane. Follow this to a road.

Turn left at the road for 300m to reach a sharp right-hand bend. At this bend take the lane straight ahead. Gun End Café is on your left. Continue along the green lane past a wood to meet the roadway where you turn right to regain the start.

POINTS OF INTEREST:
The Roaches Estate – All the splendid ridge and surrounding moorland, once the property of Sir Philip Swythamley, is now in the hands of the Peak National Park.

REFRESHMENTS:
The Lazy Trout , Meerbrook,formerly the Three Horseshoes (tel no: 053 834 385).
The Gun End Farm Café, not open during the winter.

Walk 43   CALF HEATH AND SHARESHILL   5m (8km)

Maps: OS Sheets Landranger 127; Pathfinder SJ 80/90.

A fine walk past those messing about in boats.

Start: At 935086, the Hatherton Marina canal bridge.

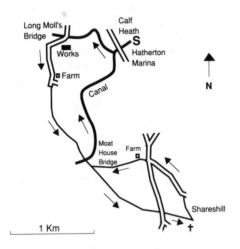

At the canal bridge join the fenced canal side path through the service area to reach a bridge at the canal junction. Crossing over, go right along the tow path as far as Long Moll's bridge where you leave the canal and go left along the road to arrive at Deepmore Mill Farm. The road ahead is now a green lane which you follow to a junction. Go left at the junction to arrive at the canal and Moat House bridge. Cross and, shortly, take the right fork to a tarmac lane.

Go right, along the lane, for 25 yards to a stile on the left with a public footpath sign for Shareshill village. Follow the path to meet another one and go right, through the graveyard, to the church and village which boasts a tiny Post Office and Stores, and The Elms Inn.

For the return journey retrace your steps through the graveyard – except that instead of going left along the path of your inward journey go straight ahead – to a stile and then cross another field to a narrow lane. Turn left for $\frac{1}{2}$ mile to a junction. Go straight ahead along an unmade lane, passing Lower Latherford Farm on the right, to arrive back at Moat House bridge. At the canal go right along the towpath and so back to the start at Hatherton Marina.

REFRESHMENTS:
The Elms, Shareshill (tel no: 0922 412063).
Hatherton Marina (tel no: 0902 790570).

Walk 44   BETLEY AND HEIGHLEY   5m (8km)

Maps: OS Sheets Landranger 118; Pathfinder SJ 64/74.

A well-marked and delightful walk.

Start: At 754485, near the Swan in Betley.

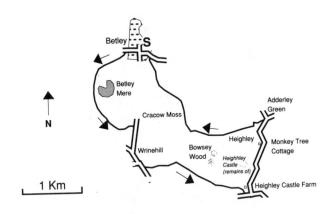

Descend Common Lane in front of the Black Horse. After 150m go over a stream and left over a stile. Cross the field and another stile. **Betley Mere** appears on your left. Continue down to steps over a marshy area. At the second footbridge go diagonally left for the corner of a wood, and across to the right edge of the wood ahead. Go over a stile, through trees and over a footbridge to an open area. Continue in a line with the stream and cross two footbridges. Go right over another footbridge and immediately left over a stile. Follow the line of two ditches, go over a stile on the right and then left to join Cracow Moss by a black and white house. Go up the hill to the main road. Turn right past Wrinehill's three inns and at the end of the village go left at a footpath sign for Bowsey Wood. Cross the field to the end of the hedge on the left. Go over a stile and turn right over two stiles and a footbridge. Continue left along the wild rose hedge, then right along the field boundary to a stile and immediately right to another stile. Go left past a ruin. After 20m go right over stile and continue across the field and over a stile by a gate. Head towards a cottage and lane. Go along this, then sharp right and left to the forest track of Bowsey Wood. Turn right through a small gate just before the farm. Go over a footbridge and up through a wood to a road. Go left for 50m and left again down a minor road. Follow this for 1km past **Heighley Castle** ruins and **Quarry** to the cottages at Adderley Green. Go left over a stile, up the hill, over another stile and follow the hedge. Go left, and immediately right over more stiles. Make for a small woodland. Go through and head diagonally left to the far corner of the field. Take the right-hand of two stiles and follow the hedge over two more stiles. Continue up the slope. Halfway down the next slope go right over a stile and diagonally left to another. Do not cross this stile, but continue right along the hedge to a stile and footbridge in the corner. Go diagonally left to the left field corner. Go over a stile on the left and cross a narrow field to steps down, a footbridge, and steps up. Continue directly across the field to the far right. Go over a stile and follow the hedge into the village of **Betley** past the cricket ground and church. Turn left past the church to meet the main road at the Swan.

POINTS OF INTEREST:

Betley Mere – A site of special scientific interest (SSI) under the care and control of the Nature Conservancy Council. Insect, plant, and birdlife abound.

Heighley Castle and Quarry – A one time Saxon stronghold, 13th-century Norman castle, Tudor castellated residence, and Parliamentary ruin (1644). The remains are fragile and should be treated with care. Stone for the Castle was hewn from the Quarry. A paradise for rock-climbers to practice their bouldering techniques. The Castle and Quarry are on private property.

Betley – Almost the whole village has been designated a conservation area by Staffordshire County Council. The church is 13th century, restored in the 17th century and is one of the best examples in the county of a timber framed church. The piers are of Spanish Chestnut, while much of the roof, knave arcades and clerestory are oak.

REFRESHMENTS:

The Swan, Betley, (tel no: 0270 820640).
The Black Horse, Betley (tel no: 0270 820322).
The Hand and Trumpet, Wrinehill (tel no: 0270 820048).
The Crown Inn, Wrinehill (tel no: 0270 820472).
The Blue Bell, Wrinehill (tel no: 0270 820425).

Walk 45   **FARLEY, LONGSHAW AND RAMSHORN**   5m (8km)
Maps: OS Sheets Landranger 119; Pathfinder SK 04/14.
A walk mainly through fields and woodland, with fairly easy going.
Start: At 078437, in Wootton Lane to the east of Farley village.

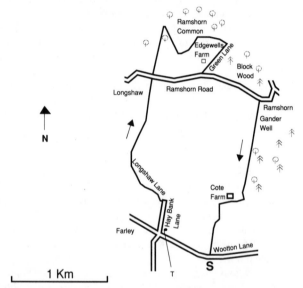

Proceed along the lane to Farley and turn right at the telephone kiosk into Hay Bank Lane. Follow this for about $^1/_4$ mile leads to a gate. Go through to Longshaw Lane. In about a mile this meets the unclassified Ramshorn road. Go over on a track into the woodland on Ramshorn Common. The path across the common is not well defined, and needs care but once Edgewells Farm is reached it becomes easier to follow. When the path meets Green Lane turn left and follow it to the Ramshorn Road. In the hamlet of Ramshorn, where the route turns down to the right past Gander Well. From this point the view is extensive: on very clear days the Welsh hills may be seen. Proceed down past Gander Well and through Cote Farm yard. Shortly after leaving the farmyard go the left down a track and cross a small stream. Go over a stile on the right and up through a plantation to return to the starting point in Wootton Lane.

REFRESHMENTS:
There are no pubs or inns on this walk for refreshment.

Walk 46   MADELEY AND ASTON   5m (8km)

Maps: OS Sheets Landranger 118; Pathfinder SJ 64/74.

An enjoyable walk with surprisingly good views and industrial and historic interest.

Start: At 773443, the car park at the southern end of Madeley near the church and School.

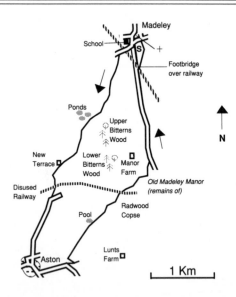

Go left out of the car park and left along the main road and over the railway bridge. Follow the Woore road for a short way and take the track on the left marked as a bridlepath. After 200m continue on an unmade track, (**Red Lane**) and pass two ponds on their left. Go through an iron gate and cross to another iron gate. Go through a cutting into an open field. Pass through a gateway to the left of a large iron gate and, keeping the hedge on the right, go to another large iron gate and along a lane between hedges. Go straight on past New Terrace Farm on your right, and keep to the right of the small cottage into the field. Continue with a small stream to your right then veer left towards a footbridge over the River Lea. Go under the bridge of the disused Market Drayton railway and through a gate. Turn right after the bridge and follow the embankment of the old waggon route to a lane. Take this lane to the village of Aston.

Keep turning left in the village until the road turns right and a lane goes straight on to Lunts Farm. Turn left at this point (at a footpath sign). Go between hedges for 50m, then right and, eventually, cross a stile. Keep the hedge on the left and cross two more stiles and an open field. Go diagonally right and aim for a stile to the right of a large oak tree, and go straight across the next field to another stile. Cross the footbridge and stile and go straight ahead, keeping to the right of a pool. Go diagonally left here to another footbridge and stile. Go over these and turn left. Go over another stile into the disused railway cutting. Turn right for about 25m and go up the opposite bank and over a stile. Take a line rightwards to a point some 100m along the field boundary from the railway bank. Go over a stile and footbridge, and make for the site of the moat and gardens of the ruined **Madeley Manor**. Go left over the second bridge and up the track for 50m. Now go diagonally right to the field corner and over a stile on to a road. Go left along the road for about 1.5km to a footbridge over the railway. Go over this bridge and into a field by a gate. Cross the small footbridge and turn diagonally left to cross the field to another gate. Go down the track and left to **Madeley** car park.

POINTS OF INTEREST:

Red Lane – This is the old horse drawn waggon lane between Aston and Madeley. Parts are still very evocative.

Madeley Manor – Originally built in the 14th century, it was rebuilt in Tudor/Jacobean style by the Offley family. It is now, sadly, ruinous.

Madeley – A well maintained village with plans for a conservation area. There are several fine buildings, one of which is the School, on the opposite side of the road to All Saints Church. It was founded by the benefaction of Sir John Offley in 1658 for the free education of boys and girls of the parishes of Madeley, Onneley, and Mucklestone.

REFRESHMENTS:
The Offley Arms, (tel no: 0782 750242).
The Bridge Inn, (tel no: 0782 750977).

Walk 47   **UPPER LONGTON AND FLAXLEY GREEN**   5m (8km)
Maps: OS Sheets Landranger 128; Pathfinder SK 01/11.
*Though on the urban fringe of Rugeley most of this walk is within
the Cannock Chase AONB.*
Start: At 058145, at the forest edge in Upper Longdon.

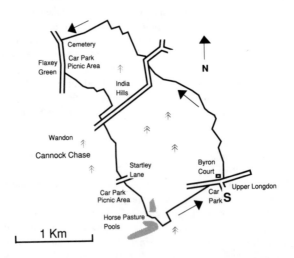

Almost opposite Shavers Lane and to the right of Byron Court, is an unsurfaced lane
going downhill. Follow this: it soon becomes a sunken green lane and meets a
T-junction of tracks. Turn to the end of the right-hand line of oak trees and follow the
direction of the small waymarker to the right. Cross a field, heading for the tree just
visible over the rise. On reaching it you will see your way forward: go over a stile and
follow the left-hand hedge/fence to, and over, a double corner stile. Continue over the
brow of the hill and go down to a stile in a fence and then further down to a stream and
another stile. Take a narrow fenced path rising up the other side to the old railway
bed. Climb the stile at the side of a gate and go to the protruding corner opposite. Go
uphill, with the hedge on your left, to a road. Go right, and then left to follow the
perimeter fence of Rugeley Aluminium Products for a short way. At a junction of

paths on the woodland edge bear right, following the path around the oddly named India Hills, until the line of the old railway is met again at the bottom of a hill. Turn sharp left and follow the fence on your right along a path of several turns to meet a T-junction at the top of a rise. Go right and down to the floor of a small valley. Turn left along the cross track to reach a road at a cemetery.

Turn left along the road as far as the sign for the car park and picnic area at Flaxey Green. Take the track, and follow it up and through a second traffic barrier to a junction of tracks on the ridge top. Go left along the broad ridge track until it narrows at a clump of gorse bushes. Go through a gap on the right and steeply down a path. Swing right at a fence and follow the edge of the open heathland. After a while go left, through trees, to the road turning left and then right through the British Coal barrier. At the landfall bear right into the trees following a broad green track. Shortly, take the right fork away from the landfill, going along a broad forestry track to meet the road at Startley Lane Car Park and Picnic Area. Go through the car park and follow the path between the old and new plantings next to the subsidence warning sign – a reminder of Cannock Chase's subterranean mineral wealth. Continue to a broad forestry road at the first of the Horsepasture Pools. Turn left into the valley bottom and, after crossing the outflow bridge, turn left and stay with this main track as it swings left and then right.

Continue along the forest road back to the metalled road at Upper Longdon.

Walk 48   THE CARRY LANE TRACK   5m (8km)

Maps: OS Sheets Landranger 128; Pathfinder SK 03/13.

An easy walk away from roads.

Start: At 052313, on the north side of the A518, about 3 miles
south-west of Uttoxeter.

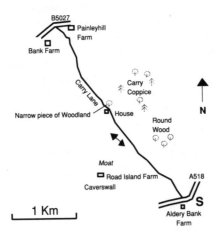

The route is well defined for almost the whole of its length. It runs approximately
parallel with the small River Blythe, which is, on average, $\frac{1}{2}$ mile away to the left.
Between the track and the river and close to Caverswall there is a moated site: no
written records of its history exist so far as is known. About half-way along its length
the track enters a narrow piece of woodland. At this point a house is passed, the only
one along the route. The woodland extends along the track for more than a $\frac{1}{4}$ mile. At
one time it was bigger. As you proceed the track becomes somewhat less well-defined,
but is still easy to follow: keep to the hedge on your left. When you reach the end of
this hedge cross the field ahead and in about 200 yards a gate is reached. Beyond the
gate the remainder of the track is very well defined to where it meets the B5027.

     Although the return to the starting point necessitates retracing your steps back again along the track it is a pleasant and easy walk. Even through there are no recorded details of the earlier existence or uses of the Carry Lane track it is highly probable that it is an old road.

REFRESHMENTS:
There are no pubs or inns on this walk.

Walk 49   THE CALDON VALLEY   5m (8km)

Maps: OS Sheets Landranger 128 & 119; Pathfinder SK 04/14.
A pleasant walk a sense of exploration on the outward journey and the knowledge that there is an easy route back.
Start: At 027476, Froghall Picnic area.

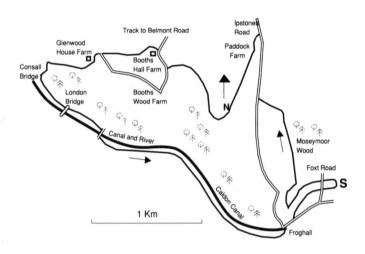

From Froghall Picnic area go over to the café and Foxt Road. Cross the canal bridge and go down steps on left along the path on the right of the canal to a footbridge. Cross bridge and turn right into Moseymoor Wood. Follow the uphill path with a brook on your right. Ignore a path off to the right and go straight on, passing a lake on the right, and then uphill to a farm gate. Go into the field and follow the hedge on the right to a road. Turn right for a few hundred yards, then turn off left at a stile to a farm track going left and uphill. Ignore later track going off right, and continue straight on to a stile in a wall. Cross into a second field and follow tracks across the middle of the field to a gap in a wall. Go through into a third field and go across this to a gate. Go into a fourth field and diagonally right to a low part of the wall and cross into a fifth field. Go right along the wall to a gate into a sixth field. Follow the wall on the right, but when it turns right go diagonally right across the field to a large oak tree. Take a wide track going down to a stream.

Cross a stile and footbridge, and go up log steps to a stile. Cross into a field and go uphill to the top left corner and out over a wire fence. Cross a farm track to a stile. Cross into a field and go diagonally left on to another track. Go to a stile in the stone wall on the left. Cross into a farm yard and go diagonally left to a gate and another farm track. Turn left off the track over wire into a field and follow the hedge on the left to a gate in the top left corner. Go into another field, and follow the hedge on the right to its end. Turn left and go out through hedge gaps to a farm track. Turn right and go through a gate into Glenwood House Farm yard. Turn off left at the barn and go through a gate into a field. Keep to the hedge on the right, but when it curves right, go diagonally left across the field to a stile in the middle of the field (NOT the stile in the opposite right corner). Cross the stile into woods – ignore the path to right – and follow a woodchip path slightly left to join a main new path. Turn right on this path which goes downhill to log steps and on to the Caldon Canal by Podmores (or London) Bridge. Turn left along the Canal (a part of the Staffordshire Way) follow it back to Froghall.

Walk 50   WETLEY ROCKS AND CONSALLDALE   5m (8km)

Maps: OS Sheets Landranger 118; Pathfinder SJ 84/94 & 85/95.

A delightful walk through our early industrial past.

Start: At 972488, near an old quarry.

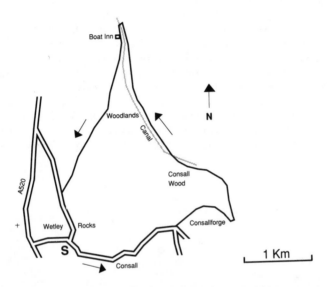

To reach the start turn right or left off the A522 south of Wetley Rocks for Consall ($^3/_4$mile). Continue down the road for 1.5km through the hamlet of Consall and follow the road towards Consall Forge. On a bend just before Consall Nature Park take a footpath on the left for Consall Forge. Go across fields and through overgrown spoil heaps, then right across another field to reach the steps down to the **old furnaces** and the Black Lion pub. Go immediately left along the canalized part of the River Churnet past the old furnaces. The Oakamoor mineral line is on your right here, and there are several good picnic spots along this stretch of the walk. At the lock where the River Churnet and canal separate, go over the lock bridge and continue along the towpath on the east side of the **Cauldon Canal**.

You soon reach the Boat Inn. Cross over the canal here and pass in front of the pub on a footpath to Wetley Rocks. You gradually rise away from the canal up to

Woodlands Farm, crossing a stream on the way up through a narrow wood. Pass in front of the farm buildings and take the lane heading slightly uphill and westwards. At the lane end continue in a similar line down and over a stream and up across several fields to reach a road. Turn left here and make your way back to the start.

POINTS OF INTEREST:

Old Furnaces – The remains, now largely cleared from the vegetation, of lime burning kilns.

Cauldon Canal – The 17 mile long canal was restored from dereliction and now has a second life as a pleasure boat canal. There is plenty of wildlife along its banks.

REFRESHMENTS:

The Black Lion, Wetley Rocks (tel no: 0782 550294).
The Boat Inn, (tel no: 0538 360683).

Walk 51   THE 'HA-HA' WALK   5¹/₂m (9km)

Maps: OS Sheets Landranger 127; Pathfinder SJ 82/92.

An easy, flat walk (but with a small hill at the start). There is plenty to see.

Start: At 972211, at Milford Common.

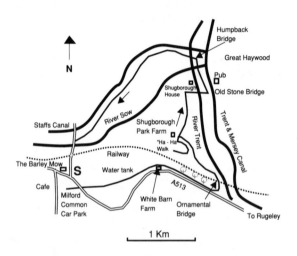

Turn off the A513 on to minor road to Brocton and the car park entrance is 200 yards along, on left.

Go away from the entrance across the car park and grass, and cross the A513 road by the entrance to **Shugborough House**. Walk along the road to a 40 mph sign and take the path off left, by a stone wall, going uphill. Go to the top where there is a covered water tank. Go to the other end of the tank and take the track which goes downhill towards the road. Veer left on to a tarmac track and go round a picnic field, passing the disused White Barn Farm. When the track goes left, turn right towards the road and then turn off left at the Woodland Walk East sign. Follow the path through the woods to reach a track. Turn left and cross a stile into a field. Veer right in the field and go under the ornamental railway bridge. Cross another stile on to a path across grassland to reach a tarmac track by a white Staffs. C.C. sign. Turn left along this track which turns right at the Schools Camp entrance and then passes playing fields on the right. Eventually you join a main track near Shugborough Park Farm. Here you can turn left and go on the **'Ha–Ha' walk** which is a path off left that takes a half circle around a walled garden, coming back to the main path again.

Resume the main walk by going along the track past the farm (where shire horses and rare breeds of animals can sometimes be seen). Take the track veering left towards the car park and Shugborough House. There are paths around the back of the House leading to pleasant gardens by the River Sow.

Resume the walk with the front of the House on your left. Where the House ends, turn right on a path through more gardens to a small gate. Go through on to a tarmac track. Turn left and cross an old stone bridge. You can go straight on and into the village of Great Haywood if further refreshment is required. If not then turn down from the bridge to the canal bank and go under the bridge and along the towpath. Barges are usually moored along the canal and there may be one going through Haywood Lock as you pass. After about 500 yards you arrive at a humpback bridge crossing the Staffordshire canal which here joins the Trent Mersey canal. Go to the right and under the bridge and get on to the canal towpath which goes to Wolverhampton. Keep on this towpath for $1^1/_2$ miles – noting where it crosses above the River Trent by an aqueduct and where it broadens out to become lake-like (to pacify local objections when it was being built). Eventually you see a luxury bungalow in an extensive garden on the other side of the canal and on your side there are steps leading up to Tixall road. Go up to road and turn left, crossing over the railway line and continuing to Milford where the walk started.

POINTS OF INTEREST:
Shugborough House – There is no charge unless you wish to see the House, its museum and farm. The café and toilets can be used.
The 'Ha-Ha' Walk – you won't see anything funny, as most people expect. 'Ha-Ha' being the name for a sunken path.

REFRESHMENTS:
Café at the start of the walk.
Several Pubs in Great Haywood.
The Barley Mow Inn ((tel no: 0785 661079).

Walk 52   **TIXALL AND HANYARDS**   5^1/$_2$m (9km)

Maps: OS Sheets Landranger 127; Pathfinder SJ 82/92.
A relaxing walk through varied countryside.
Start: At 976226, the Obelisk in Tixall.

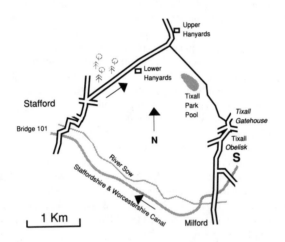

Leave the Obelisk and walk south along the lane signed for Milford. In ^{1}/$_3$ mile you will come to a lane on the left signed Tixall Lock Farm. Walk along this to the canal bridge and, going right, follow the canal towpath for the next 2^1/$_2$ miles – during which time the canal passes over the river – to St Thomas Bridge (Bridge101) where you leave the canal and go right along the road. Pass over two further bridges, and continue uphill to reach a road junction by a crematorium. Here turn right and, almost immediately, left along a No Through Road signed for Hanyards. Follow this surfaced, but peaceful, little lane for a fraction over a mile until just before the left turn for Upper Hanyards Farm.

Almost at the top of the rise, and before the left bend in the farm lane, is a gate on the right giving a view to Tixall Park Pool and the expanse of Cannock Chase. Go through the gate and head for the distant electricity pylon in line with the far left corner of the pool. On your way you will pass through two small wooden gates followed by a large one into the big field leading to the pool. At the pool corner go half right to a gate. Go through it and over the culverted stream. Turn left on a bearing of 150°, slightly right of the castellated Tixall Gatehouse. This line will bring you to the right-hand edge of a very small – and narrow – reservoir. Go forward to a gate and a lane which is now very evident. Turn right into Tixall, and spend some time exploring this enigmatic place before turning right along the road back to the Obelisk.

Walk 53   SWINSCOE AND STANTON   5$\frac{1}{2}$m (9km)

Maps: OS Sheets Landranger 119; Pathfinder SK 04/14.

An interesting ,little known walk that starts at an attractive country inn.

Start: At 134481, the Dog and Partridge Inn, Swinscoe.

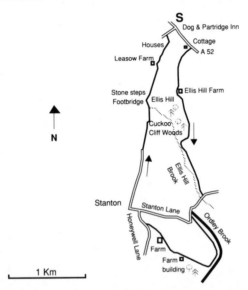

Walk along the grass verge of the A52 towards Ashbourne. Pass two fields on right, and a stile, and keep on to reach a cottage. Go through a kissing gate at the back of the cottage. Keep 20 yards in from the hedge on the right and go across the field to a stile next to a gate. Cross and go across the left corner of the field heading for a stile by four large trees. Cross and go across a field to a stile about 40 yards to the right, in the middle of the facing wall. Cross and go across the field to a stile 20 yards in from the top right corner. Cross on to the drive of Ellis Hill Farm. Go through the farm, two gates. By the second gate there is a field gate on the left. Go through and over to the left to reach a hedge. Follow it to a point about 20 yards before the end of field, then turn right and go down the slope to a stile next to a gate. Cross and go left through woods, keeping Ellis Hill Brook on the right. Eventually you reach stile. Cross and go

114

along the length of a field, keeping right to reach a stile on to a road (Stanton Lane).

Cross the stile and go right, uphill. Just past a left bend take a gate on the left to a lane (Ordley Brook Lane). Keep straight on (ignore paths going up or down) to reach a barrier with a stile on the right. Cross and keep on along the path – there are lovely views over valley and lots of primroses in season – which gets progressively muddier underfoot. Climb over a fallen tree trunk – get under the next one – and pass a sign for Mayfield on the left. About 50 yards further on there is a Stanton sign on the right. Go right and up a steep bank to a stile. Go over and right across a big field to a stile about 50 yards to the right of a gate. Cross and head towards the roof of a farm building which can just be seen at other end of field. There is a stile by a gate just to the right of the building. Cross and keep to the wall on the right to a stile in a wall just past a gate. Cross and go diagonally over a hillock to a stile in the corner of the opposite wall, where it juts out. Cross and go down, and diagonally right, and about 50 yards from the top left corner you will see yellow electric fence sign with insulated access and a stile. Cross and follow the wall on the right uphill to a stile in the top right corner. Cross and again follow the wall on the right to a gate. Go through on to Honeywell Lane. Turn right to a T-junction with Stanton Lane. Turn left and go for approximately 150 yards to reach Flather Lane to the right. Go along Flather Lane until it ends at a farm gate. Go through into a field and follow the hedge on the left. As you approach a cross hedge move about 50 yards to right so as to be on the right of a hedge dividing fields beyond. Go through the cross hedge and you should be on the right of a hedge going down the bank. Follow the hedge down to stile and stepping stones, and then follow a path through Cuckoo Wood going over a second footbridge and up about 60 stone steps. Cross a stile at the top into a very big field that includes the impressive Ellis Hill. Go diagonally across the hill, following electricity poles to a stile which is about 50 yards from the top left corner and to left of the poles. Cross and keep to the fence on the left. Go straight ahead to a stile into Leasow Farm. Go through farm to reach a tarmac road. Turn right to a stile at the corner of a field. Cross and go diagonally left, heading for stile between two grey stone houses. Cross into a passage between the houses and go out on to a road. Turn right, uphill, back to the Dog and Partridge Inn.

REFRESHMENTS:
The Dog and Partridge, Swinscoe (tel no: 0332 43183).

Walk 54   GNOSALL AND SHELMORE WOOD   6m (9.5km)

Maps: OS Sheets Landranger 127; Pathfinder SJ 82/92.

A very easy walk through varied landscape.

Start: At 828215, in Gnosall.

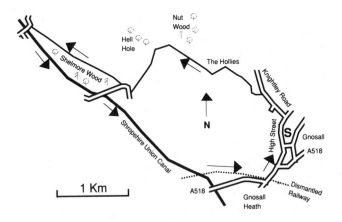

Leave Gnosall along Knightly Road and take the second turn left along the No Through Road signed for Hollies Common. At a fork in the lane go left, and at the next junction go left again down past Timbersbrook Cottage to follow the unfenced road across the common.

Arriving at a pool on the right, the road ahead becomes a track and then narrows to a clear footpath. Continue on this and cross a footbridge and a stile to arrive at a second stile near Nut Wood. Cross and turn right with the fence for a few yards to a third stile. Cross to pick up your original line. Now go left, with the hedge on your left, to the field corner, turning left and right through gates. Go over the ditch in front, and forward to a stile and hunter's gate at the left edge of Hell Hole Wood. Cross the stile and go up the slope on the edge of the woodland to cross the field ahead between two pools – with attendant oak trees – to reach a gate. Go through the gate and follow

116

a line of oaks to another gate. Go through this and follow the left hedge to a lane.

Walk right along the lane to Shelmore Lodge and there follow the public bridleway (signed at the right of the cottage) along a concrete track. When the concrete goes right to Norbury Park Farm you continue forward on the bridleway, following the edge of Shelmore Wood to reach a bend on a minor road. The last mile has been a visually pleasing one across Norbury Park with welcome evidence of deciduous tree planting.

Turn left along the road and through the bridge under the Shropshire Union Canal. Turn right up the **embankment** to reach the towpath and turn right again to follow this elevated canal path south-east for two miles.

Arriving at a third bridge – the one carrying the dismantled railway bed – take the steps up and then left over the bridge to follow the old Wellington/Stafford railway for $\frac{1}{2}$ mile. Leave the railway by turning right to a gate onto the A518. Go left along the pavement to the High Street through **Gnosall** and so back to Knightley Road.

POINTS OF INTEREST:

Gnosall – A fine village with a very old, large, timber/brick and thatch house; a stone lock up; and the parish church of Saint Lawrence.

Embankment – This great embankment was a long struggle to build. Not only did it involve the movement of millions of tons of earth, but whilst being built it continuously slipped and collapsed. In all it took $5\frac{1}{2}$ years to construct.

Walk 55   RAMSHORN AND THE WEAVER HILLS   6m (9.5km)

Maps: OS Sheets Landranger 128, Pathfinder SK 04/14.

A walk for a clear day when there are panoramic views over Staffordshire and neighbouring counties.

Start: At 084453, a side road in Ramshorn village.

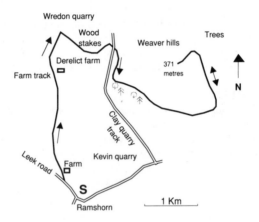

Go along the road towards Leek for about 300 yards to a squeezer stile in a stone wall on the right just before a farm. Cross the stile and follow the path across the front of the farm. Cross a stile into a field. Follow the hedge on your right to a second stile. Cross into a third field and go across the right corner of it to a fourth field. Follow the hedge to the right and then go through two other fields to reach a farm track, on the left, which leads to a derelict farm. Cross the track just short of the farm and go through an old farm gate into field. Go straight across to a gate into the next field and turn right to go through a gate in the middle of a fence. Go downhill to a stile in the fence opposite. Cross the stile and go up a steep embankment watching out for short wooden stakes going directly across your path at intervals of about 20 feet. Turn right and follow these to reach a clay track between two quarries. Cross the track to reach a stile in a wire fence.

Cross the stile and go down an embankment to a stone wall. Follow the wall along to the right until you see a stile in the bottom corner ahead. Cross the stile into a field with woods on the right. Follow the fence beside the woods to the end of this big field to reach a stile. Cross into the next field. Go diagonally left uphill to stile in middle of a fence. Cross into the next field, still going uphill, and veer to the left, rounding the corner of the wall on the left. Go over a stile further along and turn left towards the summit of the Weaver Hills where there is a stone obelisk trig. point. Stop here for a look at the vast expanse of Staffordshire.

Another summit can be reached quite easily by returning back beyond the stile and going to the bottom right corner of the field and turning right on to a path which follows along the edge of two fields. In the third field veer right to the hilltop.

To return go back downhill, then bear left through Kevin Quarry and back to the village of Ramshorn.

Walk 56   SHARESHILL AND LACHES   6m (9.5km)

Maps: OS Sheets Landranger 127; Pathfinder SJ 80/90.

A fine walk on Cannock Chase.

Start: At 944066; the church in Shareshill.

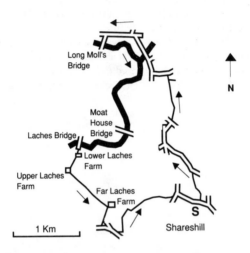

Pass to the left of the tower and go down through the church yard and then across two fields and two stiles on to a narrow surfaced lane. Follow the lane left to the junction opposite Lower Latherford Farm where a right turn takes you over a stream and on to a rough track on the right. Go right along the track to arrive at a T-junction with a signed public footpath ahead. Cross over and, keeping to the right of the hedge, pass under the power lines and to the left of an embankment. The embankment holds back a pool which is home to many waterfowl. Continuing forward, go over two stiles to reach a farm track. Follow it to the left of cottages and on to a lane.

Turning left at the lane, and then bearing right, you will emerge at another T-junction. Turn right here, over a bridge – with Hatherton Marina on the left – and then go over a canal bridge to join the road known locally as the *Straight Mile*. Turn left at the fingerpost – signed *Four Ashes* and *Brewood* – and after ¹/₄ mile go left following the sign *Severn Trent Water Authority*. Walk to Long Moll's bridge and the canal. Turn left along the towpath. Follow the towpath for a little over a mile to reach Moat House bridge, where – if you need it – you can take advantage of a short cut back to Shareshill. Otherwise continue as far as Laches bridge and turn left along the track to, and through, Lower Laches farmyard.

In a short while you will reach Upper Laches Farm. Turn left, again through the farmyard, to a hunter's gate and a public bridleway sign. Go through the gate, following the field edge to, and through, a gap in the fence ahead. Follow the line of telegraph poles to the remains of the bridlepath and a large rock at Far Laches Farm. At the rock, turn right along the farm drive to a road.

Turn left along the road and, on a right-hand bend, you will see a gated fence on the left. Go through the gate and follow the left-hand hedge for just a few yards to where it turns sharp left. Here the line of the bridleway goes half left towards a cluster of telegraph poles. If the bridleway is ploughed up follow the field edge to rejoin the line at the telegraph poles and the remains of a metal gate. Go over the fence and head for the gateway and farm track ahead. Turn right here, along the track, and then left immediately after passing under the power cables. At the next pylon turn right and follow the field hedge to a gate. From here you can see the church tower at Shareshill. Head towards it to find a gate on to a lane. A left and a right turn will bring you back to the village, the church and, not far away, *The Elms* pub and restaurant!

REFRESHMENTS:
Hatherton Marina (tel no: 0902 790570).
The Elms, Shareshill (tel no: 0922 412063).

Walk 57   DENSTONE AND ALTON   6m (9.5km)

Maps: OS Sheets Landranger 128; Pathfinder SK 04/14.

A circular walk from Denstone village.

Start: At 099407, the Community Hall car park opposite the Tavern Inn in Denstone.

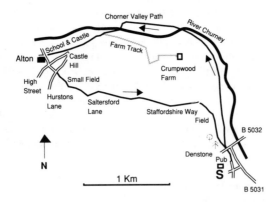

From the car park, turn right along the road towards the B5031. At the Post Office cross the road to reach the start of the Churnet Valley path, a dismantled railway route. Keep on the path for approximately two miles, then look out for the footbridge over the river to the left. Cross the bridge into a field and turn right. Veer left, following a worn footpath to a stile in the left corner. Cross on to a farm track. Go right for a few yards to a path on the left going diagonally up a bank through trees. Follow this path up to a stile on top of Alton Cliff. Cross into a big field and turn right. Veer left to a gate in the top corner of the field. Go through on to Castle Hill Road in Alton. Go right past a farm and continue downhill. Near the bottom, at a minor cross-roads, turn right to reach St John's Prep School and the site of Alton Castle each of which can be visited with permission. You can also look over the wall to the Churnet Valley below.

Resume the walk by returning to the crossroads and going straight across Castle Hill Road to Castle Road, passing St Peter's Church on your right. This brings you to High Street. Go straight across by the War Memorial and up the path on its right, passing a cemetery and coming out on to Hurstone Lane. Cross this road to stile just to right, and cross into the bottom right corner of large field. Go diagonally across to a gate in top the left corner. Go through into another large field and go diagonally left and downhill to a stile close to the bottom left corner. Cross the stile on to Saltersford Lane (a green lane) which is an old packhorse route used to move salt. Turn left along the lane for $^3/_4$ mile to where it finishes at a stile. Cross into a field and follow the hedge on the right to a stile. Cross and follow the Staffordshire Way signs, keeping to the hedge on the right until it turns a corner. At that point head across the open field to the fenced woodland on the left and following the fence to a stile by a few hawthorn trees in the top left corner. Cross the stile, a plank bridge and a second stile. Follow a path, keeping to hedges on left, until, just before steps up to the B5032, a stile is reached on the left. Cross to return to the Churnet Valley path. Turn right and follow it to Denstone Post Office. Turn right up the road to return to the start.

REFRESHMENTS:
Several pubs in Alton.

Walk 58   ABBOTS CASTLE AND TRYSULL   6m (9.5km)

Maps: OS Sheets Landranger 138; Pathfinder SO 89/99.

A classic example of footpath loss due to lack of use and neglect.
Help reverse the trend.

Start: At 835930, the lay by at the end of Abbotts Castle Hill.

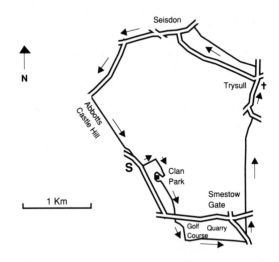

Leave the lay by and turn left along the road as far as a footpath sign for Trysull. Here turn left and cross a field to arrive at a green lane. Turn right as far as the entrance to Clan Park Farm. Turn up the farm drive and shortly bear right behind some interesting farm buildings. Keeping to an anti-clockwise direction, follow the farm road to a point where it turns sharp right to join the road you left earlier. At the bend continue straight ahead and follow a line of telegraph poles that once, perhaps, indicated a field boundary. Coming to a hedge, keep this on your right to join, and cross, a road to a gate opposite. Through the gate and upwards brings you on to a short stretch of the Swindon Golf Course. Ahead are trees with a track through them which soon brings you on to the open part of the golf course and the hazard of flying golf balls.

The path, for some way now, is totally obliterated by the golf club so make your wary way to the club road and the fence at the end of the driving range. Turn left to follow the fence as far as the edge of a disused quarry. Turn left again at a yellow course sign and then right to a point where the path is again blocked. With little alternative, go over the fence and then left to meet a hedge. Go right to two brick barns. Passing to the left of these, go to the end of the field and turn right for a few yards and then left through the hedge to follow the left-hand side of the hedge ahead to meet a road on a bend.

After crossing a road, the footpath is signed to the left. Follow this and, shortly, go over a stile and follow the right-hand hedge to another stile and a road. Due to the obstructions, this section has been rather hard going but the rest of the walk is straightforward and easy. Take the green lane opposite and follow it for a mile to meet a road near a sports field. Turn left along the road and pass the attractive **Trysull** village green on the left. At the road junction turn right and walk to the cross roads by the church. At the church go right and then immediately left – passing a thatched bungalow – and, shortly after crossing the bridge over Smestow Brook, turn left along the drive to the Mill House. This soon becomes a green lane bringing us to the outskirts of Seisdon.

Turn left at the road and follow it to the Seven Stars Inn where, early in the 18th century, the local justices held their meetings. Continue almost as far as the bungalow on the right at Little Round Hill. At 308 feet this was probably the origin of Seisdon's name – Seisdon being historically translated as *Hill of the Saxons*.

On the left is an unsurfaced lane. Turn along this and follow it all the way on to the Abbotts Castle Hill escarpment. Turn left. To the west, the walk along the ridge path offers views across the Shropshire lowlands to the Clee Hills and Wenlock Edge. A short walk along this path, which here forms part of the Staffordshire Way, brings you back to the start of the route.

POINTS OF INTEREST:
Trysull – Probably owes its name to the *Tresel* an ancient name for the Smestow Brook which you cross.

Walk 59   **KINGSLEY AND BOOTH'S HALL**   6m (9.5km)

Maps: OS Sheets Landranger 119; Pathfinder SK 04/14.

A fascinating trip into a 'hidden' valley. Good for nature lovers and tree-buffs.

Start: At 009471, the church of St Werburgh, Kingsley.

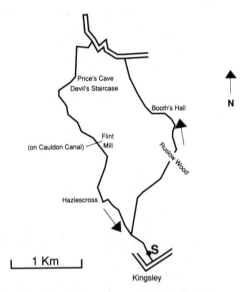

Go through the churchyard past the tower and diagonally left over two stiles into a field. Go left along the field and over a stile. Go diagonally right across an open field and exit through a squeezer in the top left corner. Continue on the same line to a stile in the corner. Go over and straight ahead to trees and another stile. Go over and follow the path down through trees to cross a lane. Go over a stile and down to the River Churnet. Go under the railway bridge and right over a footbridge and up to the **Cauldon Canal**. Turn left here to Cherryeye bridge. Go over a stile on the left before the bridge, then cross the bridge, and turn diagonally right across a field of old anthills towards a wood. Follow the path up through the wood for 50m, then turn left up a narrow path to the top of the wood and a stile. Go over and straight across the small field to another stile. Turn left just before this stile and follow the field boundary leftwards to meet the wood again. Enter the wood at an angle down on an old trackway rightwards. Go down and cross a stile and footbridge, then up the engineered path on the other side to exit at a stile. Go straight across to Booth's Farm which you pass on its right. Go over stiles to pass Booth's Hall.

Start along the farm lane, then almost immediately after the right turn go diagonally left across the open field and through the second gate on the left from the farm lane. Go diagonally left to the far field corner, straight across to two stiles and then over to the far left corner, a squeezer and the road. Turn left and follow the road past S bends into a clear area. At the next wood turn left down a footpath marked 'Consall Forge'. Go over a stream and up steps to a lane. Go left for 50m to squeezers and then follow the field edge, going slightly into the woods and down the Devil's Staircase past Price's Cave. At the bottom you reach the Cauldon Canal, the River Churnet, and the Black Lion pub. Left along the canal to the **Flint Mill**. (At this point a detour straight along the canal for 200m leads you to a 'Calcereous Tufa', a build-up of carbonate of lime from a spring in the local sandstone. Fascinating.) At the Mill cross the canal and descend over the railway and River Churnet. Continue past Raven Rocks and go upwards through the Nature Reserve. When you meet the road turn left for 0.5km, then go left again up a made-up road by a letter-box. After 50m go right through a gate and across fields to eventually reach the church and starting point.

POINTS OF INTEREST:
Cauldon Canal – The 17 mile long Canal lies entirely in Staffordshire and was completed in 1777. It was used to carry limestone from Cauldon quarries to the Trent and Mersey Canal in Stoke-on-Trent. It is now a popular leisure Canal.
Flint Mill – Erected by John Leigh, Lord of the Manor, in the 1830's, it was used to grind Australian sand and pebbles into glaze for the pottery industry.

REFRESHMENTS:
The Black Lion, Wetley Rocks (tel no: 0782 550294).

Walk 60   DENFORD AND WALL GRANGE   6$\frac{1}{4}$m (10km)

Maps: OS Sheets Landranger 118; Pathfinder SJ 85/95.

A fairly easy walk, with interesting valley, hill and woodland scenery.

Start: At 955534, the Hollybush Inn, Denford, which has a car park.

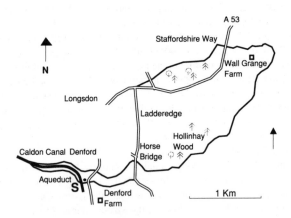

From the car park, turn right on to the Caldon Canal and follow it west until the junction with the Leek branch of the canal. Here, cross the footbridge on to the Leek branch and return in the same direction, with the main waterway below. Continue along this canal, crossing over the Caldon Canal, to reach the Leek Tunnel. Take the path over the top of this (signposted Deep Hayes Walk), negotiate the stiles and drop down to the canal towpath again at the far side of the tunnel. At the end of the canal, carry straight on, along the canal feeder (signposted to the A53) over a stile. Where the canal feeder passes under a minor road, turn right on to the latter and cross the busy A53 ahead. Take the track on the left of the feeder (signposted to Longsdon), pass to the right of a works and then bend left around the back of it (as the signposted indicates). Follow the path to the right of a pool and small stream and walk up towards a wood, keeping a fence on the left. On approaching the wood, bear slightly to the right and then cross the stile left into the wood (signposted as The Staffordshire Way). Pass through the wood out on to open fields, and turn right on to a track shortly afterwards. Follow this across a minor road (as signposted), through a field and over a stile on to the A53. Turn right along the A53 and then left down Sutherland Road shortly afterwards. Pass over a canal and a railway and turn right along the second canal (the Caldon Canal), which leads back to the car park.

REFRESHMENTS:
The Hollybush Inn, Denford (tel no: 0538 371819)
The Wheel Inn, Leek Road, Longsdon (tel no: 0538 385012)

Walk 61   **ALSTONEFIELD AND HALL** $6^1/_2$m (10.5km)
Maps: OS Sheets Landranger 119; Outdoor Leisure 24.
A fairly easy walk from a very pretty village.
Start: At 131557, the Alstonefield car park.

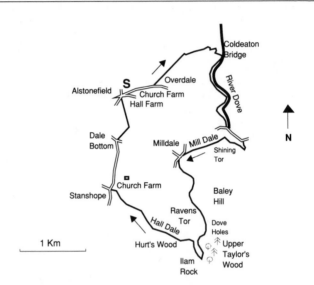

Leave the car park and turn left along the road. Keep left around the bend, passing the first track on the left and a field beyond it. Turn left along a nice track, about a mile long, to reach a steep descent to the River Dove at Coldeaton Bridge. Cross the bridge and go right on the riverside path which, after a mile, reaches a road. Go left on the road for about a quarter of a mile to a signposted path on the right. The path starts steeply, but it is only a short way to the fields above. At the top go right over a stile on to a path that goes along the wall, crossing four fields to descend to the river again at a footbridge at Milldale.

Keep this side of the river and follow the path beside the water for about $1^1/_4$ miles, passing a dale on your right as you go. After seeing Hall Dale, but still following the river, you will come to a footbridge near Ilam Rock. Cross the bridge and turn right to follow the river again, but upstream this time. The path goes left up Hall Dale for about $^3/_4$ mile to its top end. At the top, continue across a couple of fields to reach a track. Turn left on it and very shortly you will arrive at Stanshope.

At the village road go right and after a few yards, at a bend, go right on a green track $^1/_2$ mile long, to reach a minor road. A short path cuts the corner off to the road. Cross the road and take the path ahead, uphill beside a wood. Beyond the wood the path runs to the right of a wall, but then it becomes a walled track. The track reaches the road to Alstonefield.

Turn right to a junction. Go right, then at a fork go left back to the car park.

REFRESHMENTS:
Available in Alstonefield.

Walk 62 OAKAMOOR AND HAWKSMOOR WOODS 6¹/₂m (10.5km)

Maps: OS Sheets Landranger 128; Pathfinder SK 04/14.

A lovely walk through wooded dales and by streams and brooks.

Start: The Churnet Valley car park, Oakamoor.

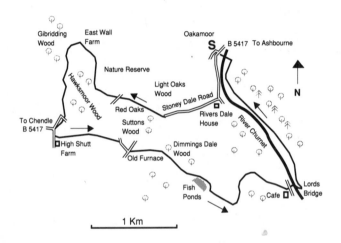

Facing the car park entrance go to the stile in the top left corner and over it on to the road. Turn left and go to the road junction by 'Riversdale' house. Turn right on to Stoney Dale road going uphill. After about ¹/₂ mile then turn off right on to a woodland track with a log barrier across, and go uphill through the trees. At the top branch right and follow the track down to a road, reaching Red Oaks bungalow. Turn left up the road and after 200 yards you will see stone pillars of Hawksmoor Nature Reserve on the right. Go through the gate and take the track to the right, going downhill. At a junction with another track turn left and then cross a stile on the left of a brick wall. Eastwall Farm is down on the right. Ignore the stile in the corner, and follow a path around the hill which turns left and then goes along the edge of Gibridding Wood. Veer over to the left to where a field projects into Hawksmoor Wood. At the top of the projection there is a stile. Cross and follow a path uphill. At the top turn left on a path

132

going along the edge of woods and follow it due south to reach a stile on to a road. Cross the road to a track and follow it to a minor road. Turn left to Highshutt Farm.

Turn left through the farm and veer left on to a path going along the right edge of two fields. In the third field bear left to a gate, and in the fourth field go to the right corner and climb over a wood-bar fence on to Greendale Lane. Turn right and at T-junction in the hamlet of Oldfurnace go straight across on a lane to the left of a house. Keep on this lane (which becomes a path) with a stream on the right for $^3/_4$ mile until a fish-pond is seen on the right. Turn right at the end of it on a path between this and a second fish-pond. Join a wide track. Turn left along this track and go for another $^3/_4$ mile to arrive at side of Ramblers Retreat Coffee house. Cross the road at the front of the café and follow a path over a river bridge and railway bridge. Turn left and down to Churnet Valley railway path. Turn right for about $1^1/_2$ miles. Cross a stile, passing a disused platform on right, and follow track to log bar. Cross, and follow a track to a pedestrian bridge on the left over the river. Cross the bridge and grassed picnic area back to the car park.

REFRESHMENTS:
The Ramblers Retreat café (tel no: 0538 702730).

Walk 63   THE MANIFOLD WAY   6¹/₂m (10.5km)

Maps: OS Sheets Landranger 119; Outdoor Leisure 24.

A straightforward walk through interesting country.

Start: At 090501, near Waterhouses on the A523. There is room
for car parking off the northern side of the road.

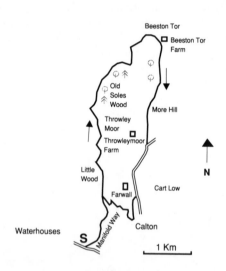

Turn left along the A523 towards the hill and left again, shortly after a 'Z bend' sign,
on to the Manifold Way track. Follow this down the valley, criss-crossing the **River
Hamps** (the river bed is usually dry in dry weather) and continue past Soles Hill on
the right until the junction with the Manifold Valley after approximately 3¹/₄ miles. Here
the track swings left and there is a bridge to the right and **Beeston Tor** beyond. Turn
right off the track, pass through a gate and head across fields towards a bridge. Cross
the bridge, which is by the **confluence** of the Rivers Manifold and Hamps, and follow
the track ahead (which is signposted to Throwley). On approaching a farm shortly
afterwards, fork right up a steep gradient, passing through a gate and over a stile as
the track becomes a path and bends away from the Manifold Valley. As a wall is
approached, head for its right-angle to the left and pass between a copse on the left

134

and the continuing wall on the right. Negotiate a gate as the wall crosses the path. Keep the copse on the left and pass through a second gate shortly afterwards. Bear right, but when **Soles Hill** comes into view across the valley ahead, bear left and walk parallel to and above the valley, heading south. Aim for a copse and a road in the distance. On striking the road, turn right, pass three farm tracks on the right and after about 500 yards, shortly beyond a farm on the right at Farwall, turn right down a track. After about 650 yards, go over a stone stile on the right, which is easily missed. Go over a second stile ahead, but at, and before, a third stile, turn right. Follow this path as it descends and joins the Hamps Valley. On reaching the Manifold Way track, turn left and then later right on to the A523 to return to the car park.

POINTS OF INTEREST:

River Hamps – The Hamps Valley is deeply incised, often with a dry river bed and contains a variety of beautiful spring flowers, which should not be picked.

Beeston Tor – This impressive limestone cliff is well known for its climbers.

Confluence – Although the river beds meet, it is only in wet weather that the rivers actually join one another. The bed of the Hamps is often dry even when the Manifold is flowing.

Soles Hill – This is best viewed from the path at Throwley and Grindon beyond can also be seen.

REFRESHMENTS:

The George Inn, Waterhouses (tel no: 053 86 308228).

Ye Olde Crown Hotel, Leek Road, Waterhouses (tel no: 053 86 308204).

Lee House Farm Tea Garden, Waterhouses (on the Manifold Way).

Walk 64 ALTON AND THE CHURNET VALLEY 6$\frac{1}{2}$m (10.5km)

Maps: OS Sheets Landranger 119; Pathfinder SK 04/14.

A varied and interesting walk.

Start: At 075426, near Town Head Farm, north-east of Alton.

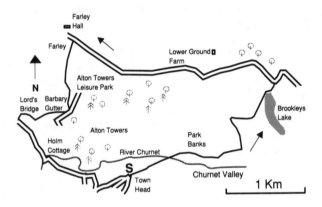

Enter the fields with the farm buildings on your left. As you cross the field veer towards the stone wall on your left. A stone stile in this leads into the woodland overlooking the Churnet Valley. The path zig-zags down to the bottom of the wood. Cross the farm track and enter the field which leads down to the River Churnet and a footbridge across it. Go over the bridge into a flat field between the river and the track of an old railway. Walk along the field for about $\frac{1}{2}$ mile to a gate. Go through across the track and through another gate. Follow the canal tow path for a short distance to the old packhorse bridge. Go over it, up the field and into the woodland. Follow the path through the wood to join a track. After a short distance the route bends round to the right and then immediately crosses a field to go down through more woodland to emerge by the side of a lake. Walk along past Brookleys, go over the bridge and then off to the left to join the Farley to Ellastone lane. As you emerge from the woodland

and walk towards Brookleys you will see ahead and in the near distance the mansion house of Wooton Lodge. Turn left towards Farley and follow the lane for $1^1/_2$ miles to the village. As you get nearer to Farley parts of the Alton Towers Leisure Centre become obvious on the left. At the junction in Farley, walk on in the direction of Cotton and Oakamoor to reach a stile on the left. Go over and follow a path through fields until it reaches the rear of an old lodge on the Farley to Alton road: you emerge from the fields with the lodge on your left. Do not go out on to the road, but right on a track that leads down Barberry Dale (nowadays often called Barberry Gutter). The lodge you have just passed is one of several on what was once the estate of the Earl of Shrewsbury. The track down Barberry Dale is part of the Earl's private coach road.

Not far down the track you will see an ancient and massive oak tree which is said to have associations with Druids. Its great limbs are supported by immensely thick chains. Follow the route down Barberry Dale and go over the bridge that spans the old rail track. Next go over the bridge which spans the River Churnet. This latter bridge is called Lord's Bridge and commemorates the Earl of Shrewsbury who had the bridge, and the coach road over it, constructed. Soon you come to the Ramblers Retreat. From here take the road to Alton. Along the way ahead may be seen **Alton Castle** which stands high above the valley on its rock. In Alton take the second turn right to the village centre. Look out for the Wild Duck Inn, and go through its car park and up the footpath which passes by the left side of the inn. Follow the path to the road and go straight on up to Town Head Farm.

POINTS OF INTEREST:
Alton Castle – Designed by A W N Pugin and erected for the Earl of Shrewsbury who succeeded the one who had the coach road constructed. The present castle was built during the 1830's/1840's and occupies the site of two still earlier castles. Its predecessor was attacked and ruined by Cromwell's troops during the 17th century, as was the earlier building that stood on the site of the present Wootton Lodge.

REFRESHMENTS:
The Ramblers Retreat, (tel no: 0538 702730).

Walk 65 ELLASTONE, WOOTTON AND STANTON 6½m (10.5km)

Maps: OS Sheets Landranger 119; Pathfinder SK 04/14.

A fine circular walk from Ellastone

Start: At 116435, the small car park opposite the church in Upper Ellastone. Permission is needed.

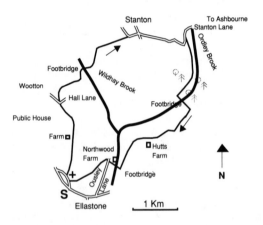

From the car park turn left up Church Lane. After 300 yards go right at a footpath sign on to a footpath into a field. Go round left of a farm and downhill to stile. Cross and go down and left to a stile and footbridge. Cross these and go uphill and left to a stile in the top left corner. Cross, go uphill and cross an electric fence. Veer right over a wood sleeper footbridge to reach a gate in a stone wall. Go through and uphill to a stile by a gate. Cross and go along the wall on the left – past a farm – to a stile in a hedge. Cross on to a farm track. Turn right and at junction turn left along Hall Lane. Pass a house and, where a track goes off to right, find a stile in the stone wall. Cross and go diagonally right to a stile in the middle of a hedge. Cross and go straight across the field beyond, heading to the right of a hedge dividing the next two fields. There is no stile, but the 2-strand barbed wire is not difficult to cross. Keep to the right of a hedge to a stile in the top left corner. Cross and go diagonally left to a gate in the middle of a hedge. Go through and keep on the left of a hedge. Go steeply down to a brook to find a stile and footbridge about 10 yards in from right corner. Cross and go right for 50 paces. Turn left up the slope to a hawthorn hedge at the top. Turn right and, at a big chestnut tree, turn left to a gate and stile. Cross and head for the top right corner to reach a stile next to a gate. Cross and along a narrow section following the wall on the right to a gate. Beyond, follow the hedge on the right, downhill and round to the left. At the first big tree on the left of the track turn right to a stile in a stone wall. Cross and go uphill to a stile in a wall. Cross on to a tarmac track in Stanton village.

Turn right on the track to a road. Turn right and go through the village – past the Post Office in a cottage – and start going downhill. Beyond a hairpin bend in Stanton Lane take the gate on the right and go through on to a green lane. Go on to a barrier and stile. Go over and on along the lane. It can be very muddy here. About 700 yards from the barrier there is a sign on a tree for 'Middle Mayfield'. Turn left and follow the path down to a footbridge over the brook. Cross and follow the path up the other side. Eventually you reach a Y-shaped log stile. Cross and go straight uphill to a stile in the top hedge. Cross and turn right along the fence to a stile in the right corner. Cross and keep to the hedge on the left to a stile. Cross and keep right to a stile by a gate. Cross and keep to the hedge on the right. Go through a gate and keep to the hedge on the right to reach a stile. Turn right and cross another stile. Go across to the hedge of a big field on the left, and follow it to a gate. Go through and follow the hedge on right until you are past the dividing hedge of two fields. There you will see a gate. Go through and diagonally across to a stile by a big tree in the hedge on the left. Cross and follow the hedge on the left to a stile in the left corner. Cross and follow the left edge, then veer right to a stile near the bottom right corner. Cross and keep to the hedge and woods on the right to a gate in the right corner. Cross on to a farm track and turn left to Hutts Farm. Pass the farm on its left and go straight ahead to a gate. Go across the middle of the field beyond to a stile at the far side. Cross and follow the green path to where a farm on the right can be seen. There veer right and cross a stile and footbridge over brook. Go up the farm track to a road (Ousley Lane) and turn left. After 20 yards there is a stile on the right. Cross and go diagonally right to a stile and footbridge under alder trees. Cross and veer right to a plank bridge over a ditch, and continue to a stile in the top right corner. Cross and keep left to a stile. Cross and go diagonally right to a kissing gate in the churchyard wall. Go through and follow the path to the left to rejoin the start.

Walk 66   **HILDERSTONE AND LEIGH**   6³/₄m (11km)

Maps: OS Sheets Landranger 127; Pathfinder SJ 83/93.

A walk through fields and along typically old English lanes.

Start: At 987351, the junction of Hill Lane and Bustomley Lane
between the hamlets of Middleton Green and Merrilow Heath.

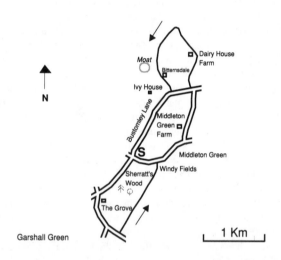

Walk along Hill Lane to Middleton Green and turn left down Leigh Lane. At the
T-junction enter the fields opposite, the footpath across which leads past Daisy House
Farm. From the farm the route proceeds along the farm track for some distance in a
north westerly direction towards New House Farm but in about ¹/₄ mile turns left up
the fields and passes alongside the remains of the large **Blithewood Moat**, then by
Bitternsdale to join Bustomley Lane by Ivy House. Turn right up the lane which in
less than one mile brings you to the starting point, where you go straight over the
crossroads in the direction of Garshall Green. At the next crossroads, by The Grove,
turn left along the lane. At the next junction fork left and then soon enter fields on the
left. Follow the footpath past Sherratts Wood to soon come out on Hill Lane where
you must turn left and in a short distance you come to the starting point.

POINTS OF INTEREST:

Blithewood Moat – An extensive site for which there appear to be no historical records as to its origin.

REFRESHMENTS:

There are no pubs or inns for refreshments on this walk.

Walk 67   MIDDLE MAYFIELD AND STANLOW   7m (11km)

Maps: OS Sheets Landranger 119; Pathfinder SK 04/14.

A relatively easy walk with fine scenic views.

Start: At 147449, on the roadside near Old Hall Farm.

From the three-fingered sign post go up the narrow track a few yards, then right over a stile. Ascend the field, swinging right to follow the boundary hedge across two more fields to reach a stile in the facing hedge. *Do not cross,* but turn right along a clear track passing through several gateways to reach Stanton Lane. Cross the lane and the stile opposite (by the gatepost) and keep ahead past Lordspiece Farm to a gate. Go through and across two fields by clearly seen stiles, then follow the right boundary over the next four fields to a stile where the hedge turns a corner. Cross this, and another on left near a tree, to continue up the field and through a gateway to a wall stile on the right. Do not cross, but turn left to go through a gateway and Newhouse Farm yard to a drive on the far side. Turn right over a cattle grid, then left into a field. Follow the drive side wall through a gate. Cross the next two fields by stiles – Leasow Farm can be seen ahead – to continue across fields via gates to reach the farm. Turn left to pass between the buildings and go straight ahead over a stile to follow first the boundary fence, then a distinct path over the hilltop from where there are wide ranging views. Turn right by the sheep wire fence at the top of Cuckoo Cliff down to a stile which is crossed on to a steep flight of rough steps: negotiate with care and use the handrail provided. The steps descend into the impressively wooded ravine of the Ellis Hill brook which is crossed via a footbridge on to a short path with a stile. Go directly up the hillside (there is no path line) through the line of trees, and then bear right to follow a line parallel to the hedge to reach a gate in the corner, with Flather Lane beyond. Follow the lane to its junction with the road through Stanton village. Turn left then right at a barn and Caravan Club sign on to Honeywall Lane. Past the fork to Smithy Moor Farm the lane becomes a track which eventually ends at a field entrance. Continue straight ahead on to a grassy way between walls (the right one broken) which leads to an open area with a clear path through ferns and trees to a stile at the edge of a wood. Descend the slightly hollow way through the wood and cross a stile at the far side, turning right on to a grassy path. Follow this through to an old blue van, then go left to cross the footbridge over Ordley Brook.

Ascend the field to cross a stile by the wall corner, continuing left along the boundary to cross two more stiles. Bear right to a hedge corner, go along the hillside to another corner. Follow the hedge and wall to a stile. Go over this and a similar one in next corner, and then cross diagonally to a gate. Turn left across Dydon Farm drive and go through another gate before bearing right to cross a stile. Go left through another gate, then diagonally right across a small fence stile to a stile in the far corner. Cross and continue ahead through a gap in trees and over a stile (obscured from view by holly trees) in next field corner. On the same line, cross the next corner stile before turning down the field to a gate hidden by trees. Through this, turn left down Hollow Lane back to the starting point.

REFRESHMENTS:
The Rose and Crown, Mayfield (tel no: 0335 42498).

Walk 68   **WEEFORD**   7m (11km)

Maps: OS Sheets Landranger 139; Pathfinder SK 00/10.
This walk takes in much of the Canwell Estate.
Start: At 141039, Weeford Church.

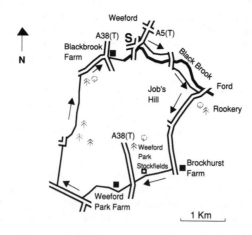

From the church go along the road towards The Old Schoolhouse Restaurant and turn right through the car park to continue along a broad, terraced track above the Black Brook. Go through a gate and continue with a hedge followed by a wall on your right to arrive at a stile to the drive of Bourne House cottage. Cross the drive and go through the hunter's gate opposite to arrive at another drive where you turn right on to the upper, unsurfaced lane and so cross the Black Brook. Directly ahead is a waymarked stile: cross and continue as far as the first oak tree in the hedge/fence on your left. Here you will find a metal part to the fence: cross and go forward with a fence on your left to a stile into Job's Hill Plantation. Follow the edge of the plantation and, after the next field, join a narrow lane above a ford. Go right, up the lane, for a little over a mile to Brockhurst Farm. Opposite the farm drive is a gateless gateway. Go through and follow the left hedge. Cross a stile into the next field and head for the telegraph pole

144

ahead, beyond which is a hurdlegate into Weeford Park Plantation. Go through to the busy A38. Opposite is a stile in the hedge and fence. Cross and go half left to the corner of Weeford Park Farm and through a gate to the farm road.

Turn right along the farm road, passing farm buildings, and go through the right-hand of adjacent gates into a field. Continue with a hedge on your left, swinging left to a gate and stile on to a track at the side of a covert. Go past Pine Tree cottage to a road. Go right along the road and in $^1/_3$ mile, opposite the second stand of trees, take the signed footpath on the right across the field and over a stiled footbridge. Continue with a hedge on your right to a gate on to the corner of a lane. Go along the lane for a few yards, and take the signed bridleway, right, to reach a metal hunter's gate. Go through this and left along the right fence and wood edge to a gate on to a green lane. This soon broadens to a wide, unsurfaced lane near a large bungalow. Continue for $^3/_4$ of a mile to a metalled road where a right turn will bring you to the A38 again opposite Blackbrook Farm. Cross the main road and go through the gate to the right of the farm, turning immediately right to go through another gate into a field. Turn left to follow the metal fence to another gate to a track from the farm. Go forward on the track, between a hedge and fence, passing to the right of a stand of oak trees to meet a cross track. Go left and across the Black Brook to a road. Turn right for Weeford Church.

POINTS OF INTEREST:

This walk is mostly on the Canwell Estate, an attractive mix of rolling woodland and pasture, which is quite uncharacteristic of the surrounding countryside. The substantial triangle of land formed by the A38, A453 and A5 roads was, many centuries ago, part of the Benedictine Priory estates of Canwell which were endowed in 1142 and came, by marriage, under the patronage of the Bassetts whose family name is very evident locally. As a result of the Battle of Evesham in 1265 the family line became extinct resulting in the estate – along with Weeford – passing through several families over the succeeding centuries. This century – in 1919 in fact – the estate was purchased by the City of Birmingham to provide land for war veterans. More recently the land has passed to the West Midlands County Council.

Walk 69   LEEK AND MORRIDGE EDGE   7m (11km)

Maps: OS Sheets Landranger 118 & 119; Outdoor Leisure 24.

A demanding walk with some steep climbs but excellent views across the western Peak District.

Start: At 997556, just off the Leek to Ashbourne road.

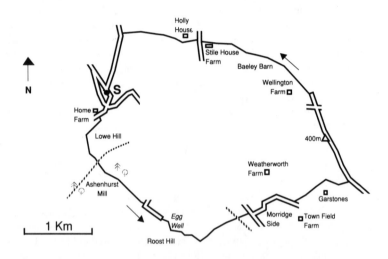

The start is just up a left turn before a bridge. Cross the bridge and go down to Home Farm. Go left over a stile by a gate and down to the left (east) corner of the field. Follow the field boundary and bear right through the next boundary down into the valley bottom. Cross the railway and go up through a densely wooded area. Climb up and out of this, and follow a lane within sight of the old Ashenhurst Mill. Continue along the lane up the steep bank and across fields to reach a well-made road which leads to the **Egg Well**. At a new bungalow keep it on your right and follow a lane up to a gate and an ancient roadway. Go along this for 0.5km until, after three gates, it is possible to go left over a stile and to cross fields in a north-easterly direction to the railway and the main **Leek** to Ashbourne road beyond. Opposite and a little to the right is a small lane which leads up to a farm and hauliers yard. Take this lane until you reach a bend with a large dug out hollow. Go left here and follow the fingerpost and lane up to where the lane becomes concreted. At the end of the concrete section go left over a stile and along the field edge until it is possible to turn up and across fields to reach the road and Morridge Edge. Go left for 1km to a Milestone at a road junction. Just beyond the junction take a turn down to the left over stiles and across fields above Wellington Farm and heading for Bealey Barn. Continue past this to Stile House Farm and Holly House where you cross a road. Go steeply down and then up to meet a narrow high walled road entry close to an old peoples home. At the road turn left to return to the start.

POINTS OF INTEREST:

Egg Well – Said to date back to Roman times and to have healing properties.

Leek – A well preserved town with splendid Victorian buildings. The industrial development of the area is fascinating and a visit to the Brindley Water Mill is well worthwhile.

REFRESHMENTS:

Although there are no refreshments on route, Leek is full of good pubs and a selection of cafés.

Walk 70 WETTON MILL, BUTTERTON AND WARSLOW 7m (11km)
Maps: OS Sheets Landranger 119; Outdoor Leisure 24.
A pleasant walk with scenic variety.
Start: At 095561, the public car park Wetton Mill.

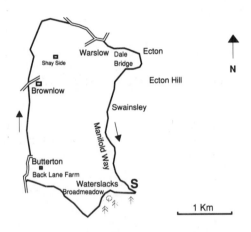

From the car park cross the road and pass through a gate on to a wide path which, 300 yards on, continues alongside Hoo Brook to the junction of five footpaths. Take the one veering right, still on the right-hand bank of the brook, but crossing to the left after approximately 400 yards. Continue along the brook to where the path ends and there turn left up the field to a gate and the road into Butterton. Follow the road through the village, keeping right at the junction to pass the Black Lion Inn and reach a road junction adjacent to the church. Turn right, then left along a walled track and where it ends continue on a straight line down the field to cross the brook (no footbridge) and the stile opposite. Occasionally the brook may be too high to ford, in which case go left along it, swinging left up the field to a small gate in the roadside wall. Follow the road up to the T-junction. Climb the field to cross a stile near the left corner on to the road near a T-junction.

Go left on the minor road turning right over a nearby stile to follow the boundary to a second stile. Cross to find a third at a footpath crossroads. Go over the stile and follow the field boundary as it swings left before reaching a rough track. Follow this through to the road at Warslow. Walk down through the village, past the Greyhound Inn, to a road junction. Turn left, then go right over the road to a stile adjacent a farm house. Cross and the one opposite and continue along the left boundary to a stile in the corner. Cross and follow the wall down the field. Turn through a gate and go diagonally left to a wall stile hidden by bushes. A clear path beyond leads to the road across which can be seen the remains of the Dale Lead Mine. Descend the road across the River Manifold and turn right on to the Manifold Trail (see Note to Walk 17) below Ecton Hill and its mining remains (see Note to Walk 33). Follow the Trail for an easy but scenic walk back to **Wetton Mill**.

POINTS OF INTEREST:

Wetton Mill – The nearby rock shelter contained animal remains of late glacial period (80,000BC) and Mesolithic (Middle Stone Age) man. Excavations of eight other caves or rock shelters along the valley nearby revealed remains of man and animals spanning the period from the late upper Paleolithic (Early Stone Age) period through to the Bronze Age.

REFRESHMENTS:
Tea Room, Wetton Mill (during season).
The Black Lion Inn, Butterton (tel no: 05388 232).
The Greyhound Inn, Warslow (tel no: 0209 94220).

Walk 71   **CANNOCK CHASE**   7m (11km)

Maps: OS Sheets Landranger 127; Pathfinder SJ 82/92 & 81/91,
SK 01/11 & 02/12.

*A pleasant walk to stepping stones and then through the forest
where deer can sometimes be seen.*

Start: Milford car park.

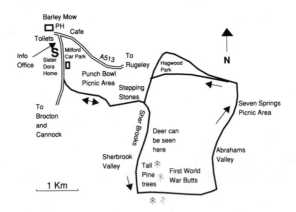

Take the path in line with two red litter bins at the entrance to the log enclosure on the
car park. Go up a slight rise and soon you will see the 'Sister Dora' Home on the right.
Keep on along the wide track, which curves down and joins another track. Keep on
the wide centre track ignoring other paths going off to the left and right. Eventually
you will reach a direction post on the left, signed for Coppice Hill and the Punchbowl.
Turn down the signed track. This joins a wider track on a bend. Turn right on this new
track following a mesh wire on the left. There is also a post showing the direction to
Stepping Stones, $^3/_4$ mile. Cross Sher Brook by stepping stones and take the first path
off to the right. This path continues in the same direction but stays on the left of the
Brook.

Continue for just over a mile to reach a T-junction with another track. Turn left, uphill, on this new track. At a crossing of tracks go straight across on the track between tall pine trees. Continue straight ahead at the second crossing of tracks, reached as you come out of the trees. Over on the left can be seen a long, man-made bank of sand which formed rifle range butts during the First World War. Continue straight across the third crossing of tracks, now going downhill. At the bottom, turn left at a T-junction with a reddish-brown track and continue along this track for about $1^1/_2$ miles passing a red 'Ranges' sign on right and taking the main path through the trees to Seven Springs picnic area. Go to the car park and turn left on the track at the opposite end to the car entrance. It has a picnic table on its left and a log barrier across it. At the first fork take the right path, uphill, and continue along this main path, ignoring any minor paths going off to left or right. You are walking more or less parallel with the main A513 road and the noise of traffic from your right acts as a guide. Eventually you meet a 2-strand wire fence enclosing woods on your right. Follow this wire back to the Stepping Stones. Return to the car park by reversing the outward route.

REFRESHMENTS:
The Barley Mow Inn (tel no: 0785 661079).

Walk 72   FREEHAY AND THREAPWOOD   7m (11km)

Maps: OS Sheets Landranger 119; Pathfinder SK 04/14.

A walk comprising country lanes and fields.

Start: At 029412, in Croxden Lane, two miles south-east of Cheadle.

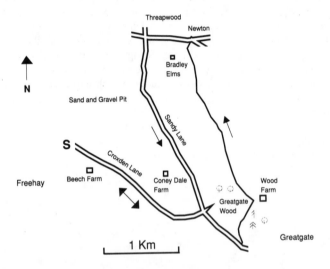

Walk along Croxden Lane to a road junction and turn right towards Great Gate. Just before the village there is a stone stile in the wall on the left. Go over into a field and take the path that ascends to higher ground. From the stone wall at the top the path crosses a field towards the woodland. The path is not well-defined but there are stiles which assist with way finding, The walk goes through woodland and fields towards the B5032 at Threapwood. Between the woodland and the road the view south-east on clear days is extensive, extending as far as Leicestershire. Also from here, but nearer at hand, may be seen Denstone College, Alton Towers and the Weaver Hills which constitute the southern end of the Pennine Chain.

As you near the B5032 road the route bears right to join a minor road at Bradley Lane end. Turn left on this road and in a few yards join the B5032. Go left along it for about 500 yards to Threapwood where at the crossroads by the Highwayman Inn (no refreshments) you turn left along the lane towards Great Gate. Follow this pleasant road (known as Sandy Lane) for $1\frac{1}{2}$ miles and turn right up Croxden Lane. The last section of the walk retraces the outward few yards.

Walk 73   **PENKRIDGE AND PILLATON**   7m (11km)

Maps: OS Sheets Landranger 127; Pathfinder SJ 81/91.

This walk passes under the M6 motorway twice, but soon leaves the traffic noise behind for a wooded, rural interlude.

Start: At 922140, the public car park in Penkridge.

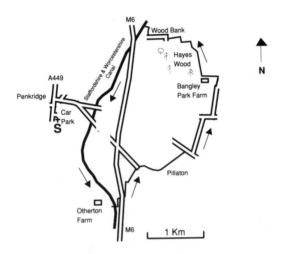

From the car park go right to the island in the village centre. There bear right, and right again at the next junction. Follow the road past several historic shops and hostelries to the Boat Inn on the Staffordshire and Worcestershire Canal (see Note to Walk 77). Go right (south) along the towpath for a little more than a mile to the sixth bridge at Otherton Lock, opposite Otherton Farm. Go left over the bridge and under the motorway to a gate, and then left across a field to an obvious fence stile. In the next field turn right along the edge for 10 yards, and then strike left across the field on a bearing of 25° (just left of the buildings) to arrive at a gate on a bend in a farm drive. Go right to pass Moor Hall Cottages and follow the track/drive forward.

At a junction turn left to pass, on your right, the historic **Pillaton Old Hall.** Continuing, pass Pillaton Hall Farm to reach a road. Turn right for a short way, then go left at the sign for the Cats Holiday Hotel along a quiet, unclassified lane to another road. Here go right, and then left along the No Through Road that becomes more of a track as it swings left to Bangley Park Farm. In this area, many of the original footpaths have been diverted and the new lines do not yet appear on most OS maps. Following the directions.

At the farmhouse the track swings right through a gate into Hayes Wood. Follow the track along the woodland edge and then left to a stile, in a fence. Do not cross the stile but turn right, with the fence on your left, to another stile at an old oak tree. Go over this and follow the fence to another stile. Go left to a gate and stile into a hedged green lane which becomes a surfaced lane on joining that from Wood Bank Farm. Continue for about 100 yards and take the track on the right, through trees, to the gate into the Teddesley Estate. Here go left to join the canal and the towpath back to the Boat Inn and **Penkridge**.

POINTS OF INTEREST:

Penkridge – A very old market village whose cattle market has been held since the 13th-century. If you can complete the walk on Wednesday, the day of the market you will have a very full and interesting time.

Pillaton Old Hall – Was the seat of the Littleton family prior to Sir Edward Littleton – the first Lord Hatherton – building Teddesley Hall. The Old Hall is reputed to have contained a secret hoard of coins which paid for the building of the new hall.

REFRESHMENTS:
The Boat Inn (tel no: 0785 714178).

Walk 74   **UPPER HULME AND BEARSTONE ROCK**   7m (11km)
Maps: OS Sheets Landranger 118 & 119; Outdoor Leisure 24.
An invigorating walk over some of the highest ground in Staffordshire.
Start: At 013609, by the school in Upper Hulme.

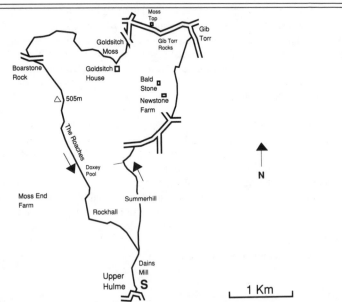

Descend to the hamlet and the ford over the River Churnet. Turn right, before the stream, up a concrete lane and follow the right bank of the stream. Cross over in front of the Dains Mill ruin and follow the left bank of the stream. Go left in front of a ruined barn, leaving the stream, to a squeezer stile. Go diagonally right here to reach an open lane and go straight ahead to a gate. Go right along the field edge to cross a stile towards a cleft valley and trees. Go through the cleft towards the farm, then over a small bridge and two stiles. Cross a bridge and another stile. Go across the field towards the farm. Go over another stile and head to the left of Healow Farm. **Flash** – at 1518 feet above sea level the highest village in England – gave its name to the slang term for counterfeit money as in past days 'coiners' had their headquarters here. Go through gates and exit along a lane to the road. Turn right and pass one junction to a second one by a house. Take the lane to the right of the house past Newstones Rock and follow the ridge to Gib Torr. Turn right between gritstone walls for 50m then head left towards the forest area and through to a minor road. Go left to a junction then left again for about 1km to a cross roads. Go left here for 100m to cross a road into a farm lane. Go down this lane and turn right for a farm. Go right 50m before the farm and diagonally down to a stile in a corner by Black Brook. Follow the old lane on the right of the brook to a footbridge. Cross this and go up the other side to road. Cross straight over and follow the wide, worn path to the Trig point, (505m). Continue along the worn path along the edge of the **Roaches** passing **Doxy's Pool** on the left. The path descends to a gap: go down to the right and then turn left under the main tier of **Rockhall Cottage** on your left in trees. Below the Cottage turn left and follow the wall to the second stile on the right. Go over this and then, immediately, diagonally left to a farm. Go over two stiles at the back of the farm. Go over a stile and down the farm road to a right bend. At this bend go straight ahead to cross a squeezer stile in front of the ruined barn to rejoin the outward section of the walk. Reverse this first section back to Upper Hulme.

POINTS OF INTEREST:
Rockhall Cottage – Once the home of Bess Bowyer, the daughter of a Moss Trooper. More recently home to 'Doug', the self-styled Lord of the Roaches, and his wife. Soon to be possessed by the Peak National Park.
Roaches, Gib Torr, Baldstones, Newstones, and Ramshaw Rocks – These outcrops are justly famous for the variety and outstanding quality of their rock-climbing routes. From the Roaches skyline, particularly in clearing weather after rain, it is possible to see as far as Cannock Chase, The Wrekin, the Welsh mountains, Merseyside, and, some say, The Great Orme at Llandudno.
Doxy's Pool – Rumoured to be named after the beautiful daughter of Bess Bowyer. She was carried off one day by strange men and Bess thereafter languished, and died of grief.
The Roaches Estate is home to the famous wallabies that escaped from Sir Philip Swythamley's private zoo during the second world war.

REFRESHMENTS:
The Rock Inn, Upper Hulme (tel no: 053834 324).

Walk 75   KINVER AND THE MILLION   7m (11km)

Maps: OS Sheets Landranger 138 & 139; Pathfinder SS 88/98.
A fine walk near Kinver Edge.
Start: At 836836, the car park beneath Holy Austin Rock.

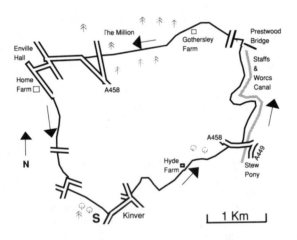

From the car park walk down to the end of Meddin's Lane, at Potter's Cross by the
church and T-junction. Turn left and right to go along Hyde Lane as far as the last
house on the right. From here you will see a signed bridlepath to the Hyde which you
follow as far as the hexagonal building on your left. There you will see a bridleway
sign pointing right to Dunsley and a bridge over the River Stour. Turn right here but,
in only a very few yards and before the bridge, look for another footpath sign on your
left to Stourton. Follow this path through woodland to a hunter's gate into a pasture
with horse jumps and go up a slight rise and over a stile into a field. Cross to a stile
and a road. Turn right along the road to reach the Staffordshire and Worcestershire
canal. Turn left to follow the towpath past the junction with the Stourbridge canal and
on as far as Prestwood Bridge. Turn left along the unsurfaced road from the bridge to
a surfaced road. Cross and continue up the sunken bridleway opposite to join the farm

road to Gothersley Farm. Go left with the road, passing the farm and Gothersley Hall on your left, to enter woodland and The Million.

Follow the path for about a mile to a metalled road. Cross this and continue through woodland for a short distance to emerge on the A458. Go right. Follow the road to a sharp right-hand bend in front of **Enville Hall** and turn left along a minor road for a few yards to the entrance and drive to the Hall on your right. Go through the entrance and up the drive as far as the Hall buildings. At the Hall buildings, turn left through a white gate and follow the road to Home Farm as far as the pool. Where the road turns right go straight ahead along a sunken pathway to another road on an acute bend. Turn right here for approximately 100 yards to where you will see two closely set stone posts and a Staffordshire Way sign on your left and opposite a road junction. Go between the stone posts, following the direction of the sign, and along the edge of a field and paddock to a stile. Cross over and continue until you see houses ahead. Cross another stile when you reach them. Follow the path between the houses to the estate road and turn right again for the car park.

POINTS OF INTEREST:

Enville Hall – The home of the Earls of Stamford which dates mostly from the 18th-century. It was extensively damaged by fire in the early years of this century leading to substantial renovation.

Kinver Edge is perhaps best known for it's 'rock houses' carved out of the soft sandstone. These dwellings were occupied over many centuries with the last occupant family being rehoused about 1950.

REFRESHMENTS:

Pubs and Services in Kinver.
The Stew Pony, Stourton (tel no: 0384 872 835)

Walk 76 ONECOTE, BUTTERTON AND MIXON   7m (11km)

Maps: OS Sheets Landranger 119; Outdoor Leisure 24.

A walk on the moors around Onecote and Butterton.

Start: At 050552, off road near the Jervis Arms, Onecote

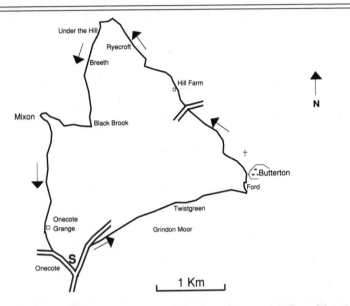

Go left along the road and turn right up a rough track 50 yards beyond a farm drive. At the first bend, go left over a wooden stile and follow the telegraph poles past the National Trust sign for Grindon Moor to cross a second stile. A clear path crosses the moor. At the road ahead go straight over and along the track towards Twist Green. Butterton church spire can be seen ahead in the valley with the hills around Wetton and Alstonefield in the background. Follow the track to its end and continue by crossing the stile near the corner of the facing wall. The way ahead is via stiles on a clear path across several very narrow fields (probably dating back to the strip method of cultivation). Go right partway down the last field, over a stile on to a walled path followed by steps descending to the ford of the Hoo Brook in Butterton. Walk up the road through the village, past the old school, now a Post Office and craft showroom, keeping left at all junctions until just past the newsagent's shop. There turn right up a lane. At the top of the rise, an excellent view point, cross the stile on the left and go diagonally right through two fields via a stile and gate. Follow the hedge through the next two fields to a road.

Cross the way marked stile opposite. Keep left of the broken wall, cross the stream and pass through a small wooden gate on far side. Keep left of a small stone building on to a track. Go over a waymarked stile on the right. Continue as directed, along a hollow-way, across a stream, up the small slope opposite and then down a grassy hollow-way. Go up the hillside, cross a stile on the right and keep ahead across the hillside to a farm drive and waymarker. Go left through a gate into the yard, then right as signed, through a gate to a waymarked stile. Continue as signed, crossing a footbridge and stile off to the right before following the path round the farm to a footpath junction and sign post for Butterton and Little Elkstone.

Cross the stile, and the one opposite, and follow the boundary fence over a stile and footbridge. At the far end of the field turn left by the wall and ascend to Under the Hill Farm. Turn left through the farm. Go through a gate and over a stile then go obliquely right to pick up on a boundary hedge. Part way along cross a stile then turn left along the hedge to cross two more stiles into Breech Farm yard. Go right and right again on the access road to a gate and waymarked stile. Yellow arrows mark the way ahead to and through the yard of Blackbrook Farm. Follow the footpath sign for Mixon along a rough track for a short distance then go left over a waymarked stile. Continue to follow way markers through to the site of the Mixon Copper Mine (active from 1730 until 1858).

Take the footpath signed for Mowidge to a rough track, turning left to follow what was originally the trail used by packhorses carrying copper ore to Wherton for smelting. At the roadway beyond Onecote Grange (Onecote is pronounced *Oncut*), turn left and left again at the crossroads, back to the start point.

REFRESHMENTS:
The Jervis Arms, Onecote (tel no: 05388 206).
The Black Lion, Butterton (tel no: 05388 232).

Walk 77   THE CANAL NEAR WOMBOURNE   7m (11km)

Maps: OS Sheets Landranger 139; Pathfinder SO 89/99.

A walk through some of the semi-rural areas to the south of Wolverhampton.

Start: At 868937, the Bratch car park.

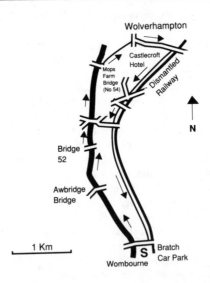

Leave the Bratch car park and join the **Stafford and Worcestershire Canal** towpath. Head north past the locks and the unusual octagonal toll office as far as Bridge 52, where the towpath changes banks and the canal becomes more industrial and less attractive. Things soon improve however as the canal feeder reservoirs are reached – their popularity with the local fishermen being very apparent.

Arriving at Mops Farm bridge (Bridge 54) cross over and follow a track that brings you to Castle Croft Lane. Cross and walk along Castlecroft Road, past the hotel, as far as Bhylls Lane. Turn right on to the **Kingswinford Railway** Walk. A very pleasant stroll eventually brings you back to Wombourne and the Bratch car park, where you will have completed a route steeped in local industrial history.

POINTS OF INTEREST:

The Staffordshire and Worcestershire Canal – Built by James Brindley and opened in 1772 to connect the Trent and Mersey rivers to the Severn. From the outset it was a success, being well placed to bring goods from the Potteries and Birmingham to Bristol and the West Country and it wasn't until the middle of this century that the canal ceased to be a trade route.

The Kingswinford Railway – Completed in 1925, it made substantial losses on its passenger traffic and fell victim to Dr Beeching's 'axe' and was closed. In 1981, South Staffordshire District Council re-opened it as a 'pedestrian' line – the Kingswinford Railway Walk.

REFRESHMENTS:

Pubs and services in Wombourne.

The Castlecroft Hotel, Castlecroft (tel no: 0902 764040).

Walk 78   **OKEOVER AND ILAM**   7m (11km)

Maps: OS Sheets Landranger 119; Outdoor Leisure 24.

A steady walk with fine views towards Dove Dale.

Start: At 164482, the car park near Okeover Bridge.

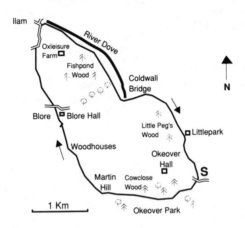

Enter Okeover Park along the public road continuing to its junction with the private
drive to Okeover Hall, seat of the Okeover family for 900 years. Ahead and to the
right is a shallow tree lined valley ascending the hill. Take a line (no clear path)
roughly along the lower right-hand trees to the top of the hill where, to the right,
stands a derelict house. Go straight ahead to the gap in the wood, cross the stile, go
along the wood and aim for the single stone gate post seen ahead and slightly left. At
the post go left and cross the stile ahead on to a walled track leading to a farm. Near
the track end turn sharply right across a broken wall, pass the farm house to the left
and reach a path along the field boundary. Follow the path across three fields to join
a walled track to Woodhouses Farm. Go through the gate, pass the farm buildings and
reach a narrow lane that leads to Blore with its 14th-century small church and 16th-
century hall (now a holiday camp site). At the crossroads, go straight ahead to Blore

Pastures Picnic Site. Pause a while to savour the magnificent views of Ilam in the valley, the reef hills of Bunster and Thorpe Cloud, guardian of the entrance to Dove Dale. Walk through the picnic area, cross the stile at the far end and angle down the field to cross a second stile and rejoin the road near the bottom of the hill. Continue along the road to the bridge over the River Manifold at the entrance to **Ilam** village. The Church and Hall parkland with Paradise Walk are well worth a visit if time available.

To continue the walk, cross the stile at the bridge corner and follow the clear path along the river, past its confluence (after approximately $^1/_2$ mile) with the River Dove. Now take a waymarked path across the fields to **Coldwall Bridge**, a large stone structure apparently in the middle of nowhere. Cross the bridge and stile, and continue downstream again on a clear path through a small wood beyond which the path swings away from the river to reach a second small wood. There a waymarker points the way over a stile to the far side. Keep straight ahead up the small slope. – take a line just right of the dead tree to reach a track adjacent to a farm, after crossing a wooden stile. Turn right along the track for 100 yards, then go left to cross a stile and field to a stile in the left corner. Cross the next field in a similar fashion, arriving at the river again by an attractive weir. From here the path goes straight across the field to the old mill building and the road where the walk started.

POINTS OF INTEREST:
Ilam – An Estate village mostly demolished prior to Alpine style cottages being built by Jesse Watts-Russel of Ilam Hall in 1830's.
The Hall was built in the 1820's and part demolished in the 1930's. The National Trust has owned it since 1934. It is now a Youth Hostel. The church has a Saxon blocked door and wall, and a Saxon or Norman font. The tower base is 13th-century. The South Chapel (1618) contains a shrine (1386) to St Bertram with 9th-century tomb cover. Paradise Walk is a delightful scenic riverside path passing 'boil holes' where the rivers Hamps and Manifold re-surface.
Coldwall Bridge – Built 1726 it carried the Cheadle (Staffordshire) to Thorpe (Derbyshire) turnpike road.

REFRESHMENTS:
The Okeover Arms, Mapleton (tel no: 033529 305).
Tea Rooms, Ilam Hall (in season).

Walk 79   SWINSCOE AND OKEOVER PARK   7¹/₂m (12km)

Maps: OS Sheets Landranger 119; Pathfinder SK 04/14.

A circular walk near Swinscoe.

Start: At 134481, the Dog & Partridge car park.

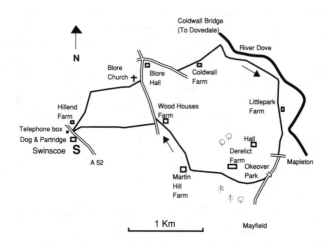

From the car park walk along A52 road towards Waterhouses for about 200 yards to a telephone box. Cross the road to a stile down by a ditch, with a yellow waymark sign. Cross into a field and farm track. Keep on the track to a gate by an electricity post. Go through to a second gate into another field. Go diagonally across to a squeezer stile in a stone wall in the top left corner, and cross into a field. Keep to the wall on the left to a stile in the left corner. Go over and continue downhill. Cross into a field and go diagonally right to a stile about 20 yards in from the wall of a small field at the bottom of the valley. Cross and go uphill, following the stone wall on the right to the top right corner and a stile. Cross on to a path going past the front of Blore Church to reach a road at a footpath sign. Walk for 150 yards to a crossroads, and turn right past Blore Hall. Walk for 500 yards and turn off left on to track to Coldwell Farm (footpath sign for Coldwell Bridge). Go through the farm and out through a gate into a field – a very big field. Follow the hedge on the right down to the River Dove. Turn right, following a worn path along the river bank. Branch right through woods at a sign for a stile. Cross the stile into a field and go uphill away from the river, keeping to the hedge on the right. Pass Littlepark Farm on the left to reach stile and farm track. Turn right along the track for 300 yards, then go left over a stile in a hedge. Go diagonally right to a stile in a hedge and cross it and a plank footbridge. Veer left to a bend in the river, then veer diagonally right heading for a stone building and stile. Cross on to a track and go along it to the road in Okeover.

Cross the road to reach a wide path into Okeover Park. Go along this until a minor path goes off right to the Hall, then go diagonally right on a flat grass path in a dip between two hillocks. At the top pass a derelict farmhouse on the right, and head for the wood railings in a gap between two stretches of woodland. As you get closer you will see a gate with a ladder stile next to it. Cross the stile into a field. Head for the end of a hawthorn hedge jutting into this field. There is also a small stone pillar. Keep to the left of a pond a little further on to reach a stile in the middle of a hedge. Cross on to a green lane. Go up this short lane and turn off right just before Martin Hill Farm. Follow round to the left to a farm track, and go right along it. Go into field and keep to the fence on the left until a green lane is seen in the top left corner of a field. Cross a single strand of wire on to this lane, passing a barn on right and going through a gate. Eventually you reach Woodhouses Farm on the right. There is a track going off opposite and oblique left: take this track to a stile after only 20 yards, in the fence on the right. Cross and go uphill to a stile slightly to the left in a stone wall. Cross and head for a stile on the right of a stone barn. Cross into a small field and leave it through a rusty gate. Go diagonally right to a squeezer stile. Cross and head uphill to the top left corner where there is a stile. Cross this, and a second stile 20 yards on in a wall on the left. Cross and follow the wall on the right to Hillend Farm. Veer left to a stile in the hedge opposite a telephone box. You are now back at the A52. Go left to the Dog and Partridge car park.

REFRESHMENTS:
The Dog and Partridge Inn, Swinscoe (tel no: 0332 43183).

Walk 80   **Hollinsclough and the Moors** $7\frac{1}{2}$m (12km)
Maps: OS Sheets Landranger 119; Outdoor Leisure 24.
A walk for those who like the quiet ways, with impressive views throughout.
Start: At 065665, the car park at Hollinsclough.

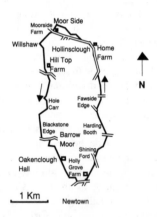

Take the road up hill past the **Bethel** (chapel) and, shortly, turn right through a small gate on to a walled track. At its end turn left on to a wide grassy path up and along the hillside. Cross a stile and follow a broken wall to another path veering left up the hillside. Go left at the top and follow the wall through two gates into the yard at 'Moorside'. Leave along the drive. Turn right on the road, then left over a nearby stile to follow the wall down the field. Cross a wooden stile, a brook and a similar stile ahead. Go left through a gate at the field top and left through another into Willshaw Farm yard. Just ahead is a telegraph pole with an adjacent gate/stile. Cross over and follow a wide path up the hillside. Go through a wall gap, continuing straight ahead to another gap between a wall and trees. Cross a deep marshy gully (pick your own way) and a stile in front of the derelict Hill Top Farm. Go through the small gap between

168

wall and house, across the front of the house and over a stile obstructed by small gate, (no problem in crossing). Keep ahead along a broken wall, then go left between broken walls and right to a gate and the road. Cross the stile opposite, go along the limestone track towards a solitary post and descend the slope to cross a stile. Follow the wall down hill and cross two footbridges. Angle left up the slope. The path line is along the wall, then veering right past the buildings on to Hole Carr Farm drive which is followed as it climbs steadily up to a road. The climb is reworded with magnificent 360° panoramic views.

Turn left along the road to a waymarked stile on the right. Follow waymarkers through a gate, then go left along a wall before turning 90° right to an easily seen stile. Cross this and two others in line before following further waymarkers along a fence to a footpath junction at Oakenclough Hall. Take the track straight ahead, and where it ends in a field, turn right to a walled track between houses to go out to a road. Go left to a road junction and turn left up Holly Grove Farm drive. Pass through the yard via two gates, then go straight ahead down the field to a stile. Cross this, another in the left wall and a third to reach a field. Cross this to join the lane at Shining Ford. A short way up the lane to the left, turn right over a wall stile and follow the wall to another stile. Go over to join a waymarked path to Hardings Booth. Turn right then left to follow a minor road to a farm track on the left. Cross the stile opposite and a second in the left wall. Go through a gate and over the stile in the top wall on to Fawside Edge Farm drive on to a the road. Go over the stile opposite and follow the boundary wall over three more stiles to reach a narrow lane. Turn left then right at the junction to descend to **Hollinsclough** on a stony-walled track.

POINTS OF INTEREST:

Bethel – Built in 1801 by John Lomas, a jaggerman (leader of packhorse trains).
Hollinsclough – Magnificently set in the shadow of Chrome (Kroom) Hill, a limestone reef known locally as the Dragon's Back. Once famous for silk spinning cottage industry.

Walk 81   **BRADLEY AND COPPENHALL**   7$\frac{1}{2}$m (12km)

Maps: OS Sheets Landranger 127; Pathfinder SJ 81/91.

A walk from Bradley, a handsome Staffordshire village.

Start: At 880180, The Webb Stone in Bradley.

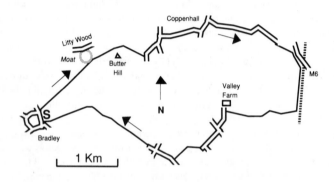

Leaving the stone, make your way to the 500 year old church of St Mary and All Saints and turn right along the road at its side. With the school behind you, walk to the end of the road and a junction. Ahead is a waymarked stile. Go over this and another double stile into a sloping field. Aim for the gate in the bottom left corner to enter a hedged and gated green lane for a short distance to another gate. Go to the far left corner and over a stile. Follow the left hedge in the next field to a farm track at **Littywood**. Ahead is a waymarker near a gate. Go through, passing two Dutch barns on the right. Go through a gate, keeping to the right edge of the field up Butter Hill as far as the double reservoir gates at the top. In the corner the way appears to be obstructed by barbed wire, but fear not! Go left along the barbed wire fence for about 5 yards to where the top strand of wire can be unhooked and the lower strand has had the barbs removed. Continue to the remains of a windmill, and then go down the hedged track and through the yard at Butterhill Farm. Go left and left again to join a tarmaced lane. Go right to a T-junction. Turn left and then right to a lane into Coppenhall. At the next junction go left, for Stafford, to the end of the village, and then right along Chase View Lane. At the second sharp left-hand bend, by Woodlands Farm, take the gate on the right and then a second gate immediately on the left. Follow the left hedge through a gate and continue on the same line towards a low, sandy embankment. Although there is barbed wire here, it can be unfastened. Continue to a fallen tree which marks the stream crossing point just before it is culverted under the motorway. Make the best crossing you can and go right along the motorway edge to the railway. Turn right as far as the next railway bridge. Turn right along the path from the bridge, to cross the stream. Bear slightly right away from the telegraph poles to an inverted corner and a ditch. The path is now a straight line all the way to Valley Farm but unfortunately it isn't stiled until you reach one on to the farm drive.

Go left to a road where a left, and then immediate right, turn will bring you to Yew Tree cottage and a bend in the lane with a footpath sign on the right. Go through the gate and over the stile opposite bearing right through a gate by a water trough. Go half left to a field corner, a pool, and a hunter's gate. Go through the gate to join a track, from a stile, to the road. At the road go right to a road junction and there follow the No Through Road. The unmade road soon becomes a distinct bridleway passing several pools to a gateless gateway into a field. Go forward with the hedge on your right. At the end of the field go through the wide gap. Go half left over a footbridge and stile. Follow the right hedge to a hunter's gate into a sunken lane which rises back to the **Webb Stone**.

POINTS OF INTEREST:

Littywood – A substantial house standing inside a remarkably well preserved double, circular, moat system, part of which still contains water.

The Webb Stone – The stone, near the Post Office where legend has it that, to avoid spinsterhood, local maidens should bow to the stone whenever passing by!

REFRESHMENTS:
Available in Bradley.

Walk 82 UPPER ELLASTONE AND THE WEAVER HILLS 7½m (12km)

Maps: OS Sheets Landranger 128; Pathfinder SJ 04/14.

A walk from the George Eliot village of Upper Ellastone to the summit of the Weaver Hills.

Start: At 116435, the village hall car park, Ellastone.

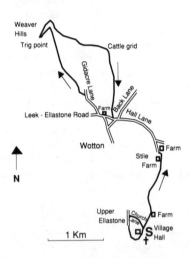

From the car park turn left up Church Lane and turn off at a footpath sign on the right. Go round left of the farmhouse in the first field, then downhill and slightly left to a stile. Cross into a field and near left across it to a stile and footbridge in the middle of the opposite fence. Cross into a field and go uphill and half left to a stile in the top left corner. Cross into another field and go uphill. Veer over to left and climb under an electrified wire into a field. Go sharp right to a wood-sleeper bridge over a brook and on to a gate in the stone wall about halfway along the facing hedge. Go through into a field go uphill across it to a stile by a gate. Cross into and go along the stone wall on the left – passing the back of a farm – to reach a stile on to a farm track. Turn right and go to the junction with Hall Lane. Turn left and go along Hall Lane into Wootton.

Go through the village, passing in front of Forge Farm Studio, to reach the main road. Turn right passing a farm, and then turn off right on to Gidacre Lane. Go along the lane, but where it turns right take a stile on the left into a field. Go diagonally across to the top left corner and cross a stile. Veer left across the next field to a stile in the fence on the left. Cross into a field and cross to its top left corner and a stile. Go over and steeply uphill, then veer left to a stone wall. At the top there is a gap and stile in the wall. Cross into a field and go over to the trig. point on the summit of the highest hill.

From the trig. point turn away from the view and go to the top right corner of the field and through a gate into another field. Follow the wall on the right to a gate at its end. Go through the gate into a big field. Follow the wall and fence on the left (but if want to see views from another hilltop go over to right) and as fence turns right go over the stile by the gate. Follow the wall and fence on the right to a gate. Follow the wall on the left to a stile in the top left corner. Cross this stile and then a second stile on the right into a field. Follow the fence on the left to a stile at the top left corner and cross on to a road. Cross a cattle grid and turn right on to open land. Follow the fence and wall on the right (ignore the stile you pass) and go to the bottom right corner to a stile and squeezer stile and cross into a field. Go across the field to the hedge opposite and cross a stone stile. Follow the hedge on the left to the bottom left corner and a low stone wall. Cross into a field. Go across the field to a gate and through into another field. Go across this field also to a stile in a hawthorn hedge. Cross into a garden and go out through a gate. Cross the drive to a squeezer stile in a stone wall. Go diagonally left to a stile in a hedge and cross on to Back Lane in Wootton. Turn right along the road to a T-junction with Hall Lane. Turn left and return to Upper Ellastone along the outward route.

REFRESHMENTS:
The Duncombe Arms, in Lower Ellastone, (tel no: 033524 242), about 300 yards along the main road from the start.

Walk 83   LONGNOR AND REAPS MOOR   8m (13km)

Maps: OS Sheets Landranger 119; Outdoor Leisure 24.

A walk through river meadows and over moorland with superb views throughout.

Start: At 089649, the car park, Longnor Market Place.

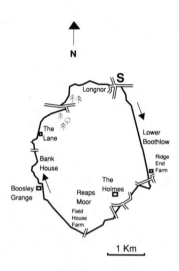

Turn left from the car park along the road past the Cheshire Cheese Inn. Go right as footpath signed into a farmyard, turning left in the middle to cross a stile in the corner. Go diagonally right across two fields and corner stiles into the meadows alongside the River Manifold. Follow the clearly stiled path downstream across several fields and a farm track to arrive at Lower Boothlow Farm. Ignore the stile in the left wall, crossing instead the one to the right of the gate. Cross a footbridge and go through the gate beyond. Continue straight ahead on a clear path to reach a wooden stile with a footpath sign for Brund. Follow this, as directed, over a footbridge and stile beyond to reach a barn. At this point the walk leaves the Brund route by turning right to cross a stile by a gate. Go straight ahead through the right-hand of two gates and diagonally across a field to a footbridge. Beyond this turn left along a track and go over a corner stile to the right of a gate. Go along the left field edge, over a wooden stile near the corner and, 60 yards on, turn left over a second wooden stile. Go diagonally right to a stile on to a road.

Turn left, then right at a junction. Opposite a farm go left to cross a footbridge. Pass a solitary stone post, cross a stile and follow the right boundary to a road. Cross the road and continue up the gorse clad hillside, following the left-hand wall round to a stile in the wall. Go over this, and another in the right-hand wall. Continue along the wall past a derelict cottage and over two more stiles. Now follow the left-hand wall to another road. Cross to the footpath sign and go as directed over two stiles then up a field and round the corner to cross a third stile. Follow the wall to a gate/stile near a barn and, beyond, go along the left boundary. Go over two stiles and a footbridge to reach a stile left of a gate. Once over, pass left of a small thorn tree to reach a line of trees. Walk to the end of these and continue across a field to a stile/gate in the corner. From here the path line follows the hedge on the left across two more stiles to a track by Boosley Grange. Turn left, go through a gate and along a wide grassy path. Just beyond the end of the right boundary fence turn right by thorn trees and cross the stream and a stile to the left in the field corner. Climb the field beyond to a stile/gate on to a track passing Bank House. Cross a road and go along a walled track to a narrow lane. Go left then right at the cross roads on to what is called The Lane, part of the old Longnor to Leek packhorse way. Go past Lane Farm and through a gate to a deep hollow way worn to bedrock by countless packhorse hooves. The way continues as a metalled road to a T-junction. Turn left and left again at the next junction. At the end of the trees turn right over a stile and right again to footbridge, seen ahead, over the River Manifold. Now head for a farm. Go through the yard and along the drive for a few yards to reach a clear field path. This crosses three fields before turning diagonally right to pass through a wall-corner stile. Follow the path to a farm access road and go straight on to **Longnor**.

POINTS OF INTEREST:

Longnor – Once an important market town. A board on the front of the old Market Hall shows tolls paid by salesmen at markets and fairs in 1903. The churchyard has a memorial stone to William Billinge said to have lived for 112 years (1679–1791).

REFRESHMENTS:

The Horseshoe Inn, Longnor (tel no: 0298 83262).
The Crewe and Harpur, Longnor (tel no: 0298 83205).
The Cheshire Cheese, Longnor (tel no: 0298 83218).

Walk 84   **WALL AND PACKINGTON MOOR**   8m (13km)

Maps: OS Sheets Landranger 139; Pathfinder SK 00/10.
A walk near the Roman site of Wall (Letocetum).
Start: At 096065, the Roman site of Wall off the A5.

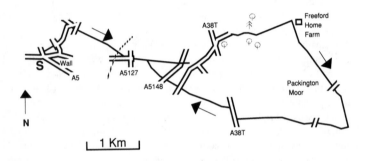

Start from the site entrance and walk up the main street as far as the Trooper Inn. Turn left to follow the road to a signpost for Lichfield $2^{1}/_{4}$ m. Turning right, follow the lane to a junction with a road. Turn right again to another road junction. Opposite is a clear track making its way across the fields, under a railway bridge, and exiting at a road. Follow the track and turn left along the road to yet another junction – this time with the A5127. Opposite are double white gates through which you pass to follow a track for $^{1}/_{2}$ mile to the far corner of this huge field. Exit over the fence to your right and continue down to the busy A5148 with the fence now on the left. At the road fence go through the gate on the left to cross over the road bridge to arrive at a pool in front of houses. A left turn at the houses brings you to a surfaced lane. Turn left to the dual carriageway (A38).

Cross and take the drive ahead – soon it becomes a broad track – and walk for almost a mile to, and through, the white gates at Freeford Home Farm. Turn right between Forest House and the Farm and continue, with Whittington barracks away to the left, to emerge, after a mile, on to a surfaced lane. Cross and take the green lane opposite. Pass a small stand of trees on the right and arrive at a green gate and a line of trees heralding a junction of tracks.

Turn right to a minor road. Cross and take the green track opposite to reach the A38. Cross the road via the central reservation and turn right. At the sign for Swinfen Hall take the bridleway left and a little over $\frac{1}{2}$ mile later you come to another minor road. Go through the gate opposite and follow the left-hand hedge and fence to the remains of a stile to the A5148. Cross the road and the stile opposite and continue to follow the left-hand hedge and fence. Change to the right side near the overhead power lines to go through a gate and rejoin the track that you walked earlier.

From here re-trace your steps all the way back to the T-junction with the sign for Lichfield. At this junction in Wall, turn right to the village church. Turn left along the church wall to reach The Butts, and so return to the **Wall** site.

POINTS OF INTEREST:
Wall – Strategically placed on Watling Street this Romano–British settlement was of some importance as a military establishment, protecting as it did both Watling and the nearby Ryknild Streets, as well as being a key military staging and supply post. The settlement also served as a resting place for official and civilian wayfarers travelling in either direction and, as a result, a significant service town grew up around the garrison. The modern day site owned by the National Trust and in the care of English Heritage, is open to the public most days except Mondays and certain public holidays.

REFRESHMENTS:
The Trooper Inn, Wall (tel no: 0543 480413).

Walk 85   **ALSTONEFIELD AND DAMGATE**   8m (13km)

Maps: OS Sheets Landranger 119; Outdoor Leisure 24.

A high level walk with excellent views.

Start: At 135548, the public car park in Hope Dale.

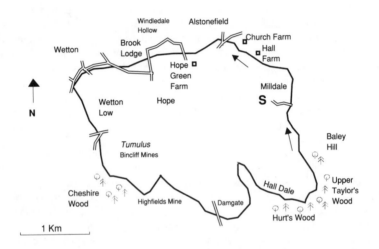

Go down the road into Milldale (see Note to Walk 41) and take a lane on the left between two cottages. This is Millway Lane, a packhorse way which crossed the river over Viator's Bridge before zig-zagging up the steep hillside opposite. Follow the lane, which climbs up the Alstonefield (see Note to Walk 41), past the Church and Manor House (1587) before turning left alongside the village green and *The George,* a 16th-century coaching inn. Continue to the road ahead and go straight across on a rough track to a stile adjacent to a stone barn. Cross the field ahead to a stile near the left corner beyond which a clear path crosses two fields to a narrow lane. Cross the lane and stile opposite to continue on another well-trodden path, keeping ahead at footpath crossroads to reach a second lane via a horse paddock, footbridge and stiles. Across the lane the route continues up the field just right of the large tree. Go through a corner stile to follow the wall left for a short distance, before cutting off the field

178

corner to join the Wetton road at a footpath sign. Turn right to the T-junction (400 yards away) then right again on to **Wetton** main street with *The Old Royal Oak* 150 yards away. Take the first turn left and pass the public toilets and car park to reach an old barn on the left with an adjacent wall stile. Cross and climb up the field, heading for the large tree at the top and the wall stile just beyond it. Go over and follow the field boundary to cross the lane at the bottom via two stiles.

Looking ahead, a clear narrow path can be seen which goes up and along the hillside giving superb views over the part of the Manifold valley and the moors beyond. For most of the year the river here is underground before re-surfacing at Ilam. Follow the path past the remains of the Bincliffe lead mines to a National Trust sign. Turn left to cross a wall stile on to a clear path through the remains of the Highfields Mine. At the footpath crossroads with the very tall footpath sign, turn right and follow the left boundary straight through to Damgate Farm. Keep ahead past the farm and through a gate, then go left, immediately over a stile to reach another in the far right corner. Go over on to the Ilam to Stanshope road. Opposite, and a little right, go over a stile and cross a field and a stile in far right corner on to a walled track. Go left, and after 200 yards, left again past a wood end to continue along the left boundary. Descend to cross a stile into Hall Dale. Walk down the dale to meet the River Dove before turning left for an attractive walk along the river, where, on quiet days you may see dippers. The large caves, Dove Holes, were created by ancient river systems. Finally the path leaves the river continuing clearly across fields and through a wood to reach a short, steep descent to Milldale.

POINTS OF INTEREST:

Wetton – This village has Saxon origins. The church has a 14th-century tower, though the remainder is 19th-century. Some of the village houses date from the 16th and 17th centuries.

REFRESHMENTS:

The George Inn, Alstonefield (tel no: 033527 205).
Shop and Tea Rooms, Alstonefield.
The Old Royal Oak, Wetton (tel no: 033527 287).

Walk 86   DEEP DALE AND CHEE DALE $8^1/_2$m (14km)

Maps: OS Sheets Landranger 119; Outdoor Leisure 24.

A varied walk on lanes and field paths.

Start: At 138732, Millers Dale Station.

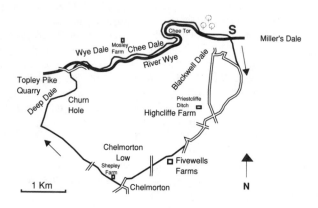

Walk away from the car park entrance along the High Peak Trail to the end of the old platforms, where there is a signpost. Take a path, left, down to the River Wye and a gate/stile giving access to a road. Go right to cross a bridge, then right up the road for 25 yards, (just past a de-restriction sign) and turn left up a path. There is no footpath sign, but soon there is a Nature Reserve notice. Soon you come to a footpath sign and a steep, stepped path up the hillside on the right. This is the shortest way to the top, but there is a slightly easier way take the concessionary path to a gate go through the gap at the side and turn right up a flight of steps. At the top of the steps turn right on to a level path which, in about five minutes, brings you to a seat (very well placed!) where the two paths join. Continue up the path to the top, (only a short bit now), and a stile into a field. Cross the field to a stile in the top left-hand corner by a gate and a tree. Take the same line across two more fields, the stiles are obvious, to reach a bend in a track. Go right on the track and follow it to a lane. Turn left up this lane: after $^1/_2$ mile it joins a road on a bend. Keep ahead for a few yards to a crossroads. Turn right and walk to the main A6. Across the road is the Waterloo Hotel. Cross the road and go up the track between the hotel and its car park, (Sough Lane). After about $^1/_2$ mile go round a hairpin bend and just beyond it go over a stile on the right to a path by Fivewells Farm. Two fields past the farm cross another track and take the path to Chelmorton. As you near Chelmorton the path becomes a track: keep left and go down between the church and the Church Inn to a road junction. Turn right on a signposted track by Shepley Farm, to a lane. Go left, then right on to another track for $^3/_4$ mile to a junction of tracks. Turn sharp left and after a few yards go right over a stile to a path across fields to the edge of Deep Dale. The path runs steeply down beside a cave into the dale bottom.

In the dale go right for about a mile. This way is a bit rough in places and slightly marred by the working quarry at the end, but is a grand valley. Cross the A6 – with care, its three lanes here – and reach the Wye Dale car park. Turn right along the car park on a track, following the river along Wye Dale for about $^1/_2$ mile. At the end of the dale there is a footbridge beside a ford. Cross towards a row of cottages and, at the other side, turn right along a path to Chee Dale. Soon, at an old railway bridge, a sign points the way to the Monsal Trail for the easier, and wet weather, way through the dale: it is well signposted and only a short diversion. A more exciting, and better way is to continue forward at the sign, on the path beside the river. But DO NOT go on if the river is in flood because in one place the path goes into the water: there are stepping stones but if they are awash it could be dangerous.

Whichever way you go the two paths come together again with the last half mile or so of glorious Chee Dale to be walked. When you have emerged from the high rocky sides of the dale, and are clear of the trees keep forward, still following the river across an open grassy area. Pass a footbridge and a tempting path on the left to Wormhill, (that's on another walk) and continue beside the water, through Millers Dale, for about $^3/_4$ mile. Soon you reach the gate on to the road you saw at the start of the walk. Go over the stile, left, and up the path back to the old station platforms. Go right to the car park.

REFRESHMENTS:
The Church Inn , Chelmorton (tel no: 0298 85319).

Walk 87   BRINDLEY VALLEY   9m (14.5km)

Maps: OS Sheets Landranger 127 & 128; Pathfinder SJ 81/91 &
SK 01/11.

A thought-provoking walk.

Start: At 983154, the Commonwealth Cemetery.

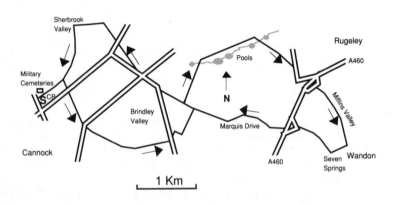

From the cemetery continue along the service road to the entrance of the German
Cemetery. Opposite are some steps which you climb to reach, and follow, a path
through woodland to a road. Cross over and follow the same line on a path through
trees to a second road. Go through the car park opposite and, passing over a vehicle
barrier, continue for a few yards to a junction of tracks. Here take the track to the right
of a signed blue route (13) and gradually drop down Brindley Valley to a small car
park and road. Go left along the road for 80 yards and turn right along the road signed
for the Picnic Area. At the top bear right – passing the Disabled Picnic Area – and
then go left through a barrier and follow the grass covered tarmac path up to the T-
junction with the perimeter tarmac. Cross the perimeter, bearing very slightly left, to
a gap in the trees and Marquis Drive. For the last ¹/₂ mile you have been crossing the

former RAF Hednesford Training Camp – familiar to many a National Serviceman.

Turn left along Marquis Drive for a short way and then go right down a track, following the power line, to the valley bottom and a pool on your left. At the track junction go right, to pass the Forestry Commission Nature Reserve sign, and then passing a series of pools to arrive at a track T-junction. Go right and cross Stony Brook by a footbridge over the ford and continue along the wide forestry road to reach terraced houses and a road. Turn right along the road to its junction with the A460 which you cross to go right, down a service road, and then left into Miflins Valley.

Walk through the valley, and at the top of a slight rise take the lesser track on the right to meet a major cross track. Turn right and in a short while you will see a small pool on the left of a right bend. This is the whimsically named Seven Springs which has a short, but interesting history.

Continuing along the track, cross the A460 and the level crossing, and ascend Marquis Drive which progresses – or degenerates according to your point of view – from path to track to tarmac during the $1^{1}/_{2}$ miles until a road is reached. Go right to a fingerpost and cross to the Birches Valley road sign. Slightly right of this sign is a footpath between trees: follow it – over two cross tracks – to the road called Penkridge Bank. Go through the vehicle barrier opposite to follow the edge of the heathland and forestry down to a track junction. Turn left to the Sherbrook Valley and then left again – back to the stillness.

POINTS OF INTEREST:
During the 1914-18 War Cannock Chase was one vast British and Commonwealth training camp. During this period a major epidemic decimated the trainees and the first cemetery at the start of this walk contains graves of many of the victims. The second cemetery – the German Military Cemetery – contains the graves of participants from both conflicts. Strategically placed between the Cemeteries is the Peace Vista.

Walk 88   KINGS BROMLEY AND ALREWAS   9m (14.5km)

Maps: OS Sheets Landranger 128; Pathfinder SK 01/11.
A level walk through the Trent valley water meadows.
Start: At 128175, a lay by on the A515.

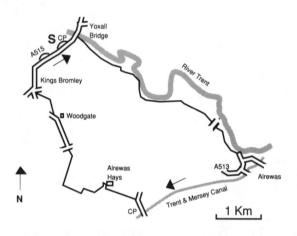

From the lay by walk to the traffic lights on Yoxall bridge and cross the fence right to
follow the River Trent downstream over two stiles. Where the river goes into a left
bend, take a stile at the side of a double gate and follow the green lane to two gates on
the left. Here the path has been slightly diverted from that shown on the Pathfinder
map, so go through the second gate and follow the hedge on the left to a stile and gate
in the field corner. Now follow the right-hand hedge/fence to a protruding corner and
from there go across the field to meet the river bank and a stiled footbridge. Go over
three stiles along the riverside, the last one taking you on another slight diversion:
over this stile you leave the river and follow the hedge on the right, keeping with it as
it veers slightly right, to reach another protruding corner where you go straight across
the field to a stile in the corner – to the left can be seen Wychnor Hall and Park.
Continue with a hedge on your left to a cross ditch. Go half right to a gate and stile.

Turn right along the green lane for a few yards to a gate on the left with almost next to it, a plank bridge and stile. Cross the stile and go slightly right, through a break in the hedge, to and through a gateway and on to a second which is in line with Alrewas church tower. You are now on a just distinguishable track: follow half right over a ditch and through a gate. Swing left with the ditch to another gate where you almost meet the river again. In the next field go half right to the far right corner. Turn left along the fenced path to a cul-de-sac. Turn right to the junction with Church Road and then left to pass the church, continuing through **Alrewas**, to the canal bridge.

At the canal bridge turn right along the towpath and follow it for almost 2 miles to the road at Keepers Lock. Turn right along the road and on a right bend go left between the houses and along the concrete farm road to reach Alrewas Hays Farm. Follow the drive to the right and rear of the house, and then go left between outbuildings to a T-junction with a track. Turn left along the track to reach a pool on the left. There turn right down to a sleeper bridge over a brook. Cross the brook and continue straight ahead across and up the field to a hedge. Go left with the hedge to the entrance of a green lane on the right. Follow this very pleasant lane forward and right to join a tarmac lane. Continue forward again to a left bend in the lane at Woodgate. Directly ahead is a stile: cross this, and two subsequent ones, towards a pylon and there go half left to a stile at the goal posts in a playing field. Now go diagonally right to the far right corner of the field and exit on to a road, via a stile at a public footpath sign. Turn right to the A515 and right, through Kings Bromley with its reservoir, back to the lay by.

POINTS OF INTEREST:

Alrewas – A restful place with some interesting timbered and thatched buildings. On the edge of the village the River Trent actually joins the Trent and Mersey Canal which, with the Mill Race joining the two at another point, forms an island. The importance of water power to the village's past is very evident.

Walks 89 & 90 FROGHALL AND CONSALL   9m (14.5km) or 11m (17.5km)

Maps: OS Sheets Landranger 119 & 128; Pathfinder SK 04/14.

An easy, but interesting, walk along the Caldon Canal. The longer option goes to the new Consall Nature Park.

Start: At 027476, Froghall Picnic area.

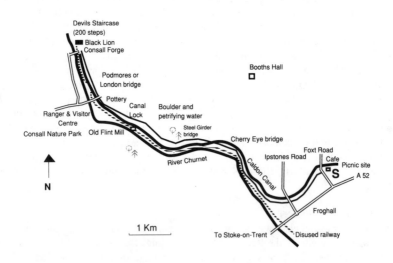

From Froghall Picnic area, with the canal and café on your right cross Foxt road on to a path leading to the left side of the Caldon Canal. Continue along the path when the canal disappears into a tunnel and cross Ipstone road to reach a path to the right of a factory, and on left of canal again. Keep to the path, the view widening to include the River Churnet down to the left and wooded banks on either side. After approximately 1 mile you reach **Cherryeye Bridge.** Continue along the canal to a steel girder bridge and use it cross to the other side. Look out for the petrifying water which runs over a jutting boulder and turns any objects left in it to stone! You pass an old flint mill across the canal and then a canal lock. Continue along the canal to reach the **Pottery Workshop.**

Beyond the Pottery the canal runs very close to the now-disused railway line – so close that the railway waiting room, as you can see from the remains, was overhanging the canal! A little further on, the valley widens out and the canal and river join at Consall Forge where there is a small pub, the Black Lion. There are usually a few barges moored here and sometimes the pub arranges various activities such as mock battles so there are generally quite a few visitors about.

If you want to go on to the **Consall Nature Park** cross the two bridges over the canal and river, and turn left along the track. Where it joins a wider track turn right, uphill, and continue almost to the top where a tarmac drive leads down to the Nature Park Ranger Centre. Here maps and guides can be obtained but the walks are way-marked – the green one being a short walk round two very large pools, and the red one being a longer one through extensive woods of the Consall Valley.

To return to Froghall go back along the same route.

POINTS OF INTEREST:
Cherryeye Bridge – said to be so-called because the eyes of local miners were reddened by iron ore dust.
Pottery Workshop – sells hand-made pottery and refreshments.
Consall Nature Reserve – one of Britain's newest Nature Parks, opened in 1990.

REFRESHMENTS:
The Pottery Workshop.
The Black Lion Inn, Consall Forge (tel no: 0782 550294).

Walk 91   WHEATON ASTON AND MITTON   9m (14.5km)

Maps: OS Sheets Landranger 127; Pathfinder SJ 81/91.

A fine country walk where kingfisher and heron sightings are common on the canal.

Start: At 852126, the Hartley Arms, Wheaton Aston.

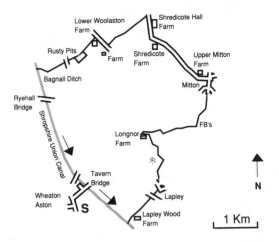

From the Hartley Arms cross the Tavern Bridge and walk south-east along the Shropshire Union Canal towpath. At the third bridge leave the canal and go left through Lapley Wood Farm, and follow the Staffordshire Way signs into Lapley. Turn left along the road and just past the church you will see a public bridleway sign on your right pointing through a gate just left of the drive to Lapley Manor. Go through the gate, forward into a dip, and left to a gateway with crosspoles. Go over or under, and forward to the corner of a stand of trees. Continue to the end of the next field where there is a Staffordshire Way sign. Go left with the sign to double hunter's gates on the right and through them into another field. Go diagonally left to a sign, next to a stile and gate, and to the right of a large oak tree. Do not go over the stile, but continue along the left-hand hedge, following the Staffordshire Way sign, to the gate into

188

Longnor Farm. Turn right, again with the Staffordshire Way sign, to reach a stile and hunter's gate on your left. Go over, bearing right to a gap in the fence and trees to reach another stile and hunter's gate. Go through and continue with the hedge on your left. In the corner of this field go through a Staffordshire Way hunter's gate to cross Bickford Meadows – an Area of Scientific Interest under the care of Penkridge Naturalists – partly by duckboards over the marshier part of the wetlands. Cross two footbridges to reach the distinctive track into Mitton.

From the road at Mitton go forward to cross a small bridge and turn left along a quiet surfaced lane for almost $1\frac{1}{2}$ miles to Shredicote Hall Farm. Just beyond the farm the lane turns sharp right, but you go left along a hedged, unsurfaced green lane. Soon the lane ends at two adjacent gates: go through the left-hand one to follow the right-hand hedge to a second gate. Go through to reach a third. In the next field cross to the hunter's gate and footbridge over Church Eaton Brook. Continue across the next field with the hedge on your left to a stile and plank footbridge. Cross and walk along the edge of the next field to the lane opposite White House Cottage.

Turn right along the lane as far as Lower Woolaston Farm where, just beyond, a left turn along a hedged green lane will bring you to Rusty Pits. Go forward on the track with the hedge on your right to reach a lane. Cross over and go forward on a short green lane into a field. Walk with the hedge on your left to the final field before the trees at Bagnallditch. Here go half right to a gate on the edge of the trees. Through the gate is a path to a canal bridge. Go left (south) along the towpath back to the Hartley Arms and Wheaton Aston.

REFRESHMENTS:
The Hartley Arms, Wheaton Aston (tel no: 0785 840232).

Walk 92   **THE TRENT AND MERSEY CANAL** $9^1/_2$m (15km)
Maps: OS Sheets Landranger 128; Pathfinder SK 01/11.
A fine, historical walk.
Start: At 152128, on Worthington Road near Fradley Airfield.

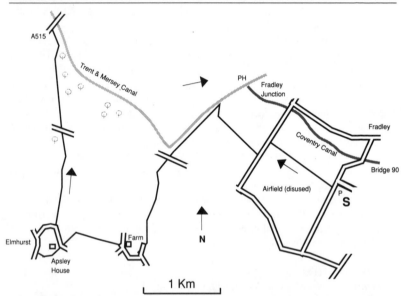

Entering the airfield perimeter at the gap opposite Worthington Road, turn left for a
few yards to reach an overgrown concrete patch on the left. Stop here, turn right and
to walk straight across the airfield, bearing 300°, slightly left of a chimney stack that
can be seen above the trees in the far distance, to reach the opposite hedge. In the lane
beyond turn left as far as an abandoned concrete hut and then go right along the
concreted track to reach a sharp right bend before a gate. Go straight ahead and through
the gate to follow the woodland fence on the left. Swing right through a gap between
the trees. Now go left to meet the canal and turn left again to follow the canalside
footpath on the opposite bank to the towpath.

　　Cross a stile and follow the woodland edge and canalside, and then a field edge,
to a road. Cross over the stile opposite and follow the field edge to a fence over which
– and after crossing a tarmac strip – go slightly left to a stile and footbridge into scrub

woodland. Over the footbridge there is a chain link fence: go left with the fence for some distance to emerge from the scrub at a stile into a field. Cross the field by following the telegraph poles to the white house so as to arrive at the left corner of the garden fence. At this point go for a gate – in line with a pylon – and go right on to a gravel track to emerge at the road by Curborough Hall Farm. Cross the road and go through the gate where the line of your path is to the protruding field corner next to the pylon. At this point continue with the hedge on your right and at the next corner go straight ahead and over a stile to follow the hedge. Aim for the stile over the railway line. On the other side go straight up the field to pass to the left of Apsley House and go along the track to a T-junction. Go right, and then right again through the sleepy hamlet of Elmhurst as far as the letter box. Turn right along Nash Lane and at the bottom go left through the field gate opposite the small water treatment plant. Follow the right hedge back to the railway line and go over it into a large field. Go half left towards a hurdle stile. Follow the same line across several stiles – and through gates – for $^1/_2$ mile to meet the road to the right of a bungalow.

Across the road, and slightly left, is a track to Ravenshaw House which you follow into woodland, which consists mainly of mature oaks. Where the track goes right, carry on along a grassy path on the woodland edge to a gate. Go through the gate and forward to meet the A515. Go right to a canal bridge. Go right along the canal towpath for $2^1/_2$ miles to arrive at the Swan Inn at Fradley Junction. Cross over a hump bridge to follow the Coventry Canal arm right to Fradley Bridge (Bridge 90) where you leave the canal to go right along the lane back to your starting point.

REFRESHMENTS:
The Swan Inn, Fradley Junction (tel no: 0283 790330).

Walk 93   **ALSTONEFIELD TO ECTON HILL**   10m (16km)
Maps: OS Sheets Landranger 119; Outdoor Leisure 24.
A fairly testing, mainly high level walk with magnificent views.
Start: At 131556, the public car park Alstonefield.

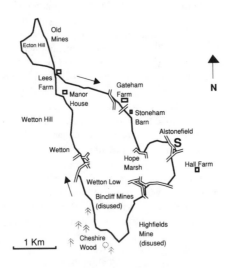

Turn right from the car park, right again at the road junction, then left at a T-junction
and immediately left again on a track by a house side. Where this swings right go over
a stile and follow the boundary wall. At the field end the path turns right, still following
the wall and descends steeply to the road in Hope Dale. Go right for about 300 yards,
then left over a stile by a footpath sign into a little valley. Follow the path almost to
the valley top, then turn sharply right up the slope to a stile. Cross this, and the one
over the road, and follow the wall up the field. Go over two stiles before angling
slightly left to pick up a clear path ascending the field along a wall to arrive at a
narrow track and a very tall footpath sign. Cross straight over on a clear path (signed
Castern) by the remains of Highfield lead mines to a wall stile. Go over and turn right
along a narrow, worn path traversing the hillside past the ruins of Bincliffe mines and
finally descending to a narrow lane via a stile. Go over the stile opposite and follow

the wall up the field. Cross the stile at the top then head for the far right corner to a stile and the road into Wetton (see Note to Walk 85).

Turn right along the road, going past the public toilets and car park. Go left at the T-junction, up the main street past *The Old Royal Oak*. Leave the road at the sharp left turn by the 16th-century farm house to follow the track marked Ecton. At the end of the track, by a small reservoir, go over the wall stile ahead and over the slight rise to reach a clear path descending along the side of the hill. Cross a small field via stiles, arriving finally at a small stream in the valley bottom. The nearby house is Pepper's Inn once used by the miners from Ecton Hill.

Cross a second footbridge and stile on to an access road which is followed to a fork: take the left branch. After 50 yards turn right through a gate and go along a well worn path to the ruins of a lead mine, one of some 70 lead and copper mines on Ecton Hill during the period from the 17th to the 19th centuries. The path continues through the ruins. Go over a stile, then slightly right to a stile by the broken wall, corner. Cross and follow the wall on what becomes a wide grass path to reach a stone barn. From the barn, once part of the engine house of the Ecton Copper Mine (see Note to Walk 33), turn left down a grassy path to reach further ruins. Take the narrow path, clearly seen ahead, up the hillside and over the ridge to reach a line of trees. Turn left along the trees, go over a stile and then follow the wall straight ahead to a gate in the field corner. Go through and diagonally left through two fields before turning left along the wall to reach the farm road via a gate. Turn right and follow the road to a small spinney just beyond the fork. A clear path descends through the trees and then diagonally across the following field before continuing ahead in a straight line along the left side of the hill to arrive at a wall stile. Cross this and the small field to reach a road close to a small tree plantation.

Turn right for 100 yards, then left on to Gateham Farm drive, immediately turning right across a field to a stile in the top left corner. Cross this and two more ahead to reach another in the left wall just beyond Stoneham Barn. Go over, turn right and, keeping to the left of the boundary walls, cross a succession of stiles to reach a barn. From there the path goes diagonally across two fields to reach a narrow lane. About 100 yards to the left go left over a stile and follow the wall on a reasonably clear path which swings right to end at the road in Alstonefield. The car park is 200 yards to the right.

REFRESHMENTS:
The George, Alstonefield (tel no: 033527 205).
The Old Royal Oak, Wetton (tel no: 033527 287).

Walk 94 THE ROACHES 10m (16km)

Maps: OS Sheets Landranger 118 & 119; Outdoor Leisure 24.

A gritstone ridge and moorlands walk with magnificent wide ranging views.

Start: At 004621, the roadside car park, adjacent to The Roaches.

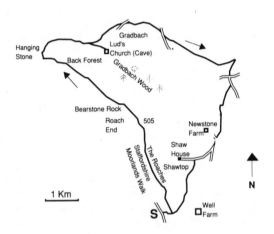

Go through the small gate at the roadside and turn right to follow the path to a stile in the right-hand wall. Take the path opposite which climbs the hillside before continuing along the foot of **The Roaches**. At the end of the rock face, turn right up a clear path to reach the ridge summit. Continue on a steady ascent to a height (Trig point) of 505 metres, with wide and extensive views over the Cheshire Plain and Staffordshire Moorlands, before descending to the narrow road at Roach End. Cross the road and the stile opposite, and go straight ahead on a clear path for approximately 1 mile to reach a stile at a footpath crossroads. Go over the stile and turn right on the old packhorse way from Danebridge to Gradbach Mill (now a Youth Hostel). Where the path forks, go right for 150 yards to visit **Lud's Church**, then return to the fork and continue descending to cross Black Brook by the footbridge.

Go over the adjacent wall stile and along the path to the Gradbach YHA, formerly a mill and built in 1785. Go through the yard, up the drive, across the road junction and along the farm drive. Pass around the right-hand side of the house and go through a gate to follow the left-hand wall to a corner stile. Go over and follow a wall. At its end swing right down the field to cross a stile/footbridge in the field corner. Cross the field and a wall stile just right of a house to reach a road.

Turn right and after 80 yards turn left over a stile and another in the wall ahead before crossing the field beyond on to a walled track. Follow this past a barn and go along a rough path to a minor road. Go straight across, past the house, through a gate and follow the path along the fence to a wooden fence stile. Cross and keep ahead along the wall to a gate, beyond which the path line is straight ahead to reach a farm road. Turn right and follow it to a road junction. Go down the road opposite for 100 yards, then turn right on a wide path through trees to continue on a clear path across moorland to a wall gap adjacent a large rocky outcrop. Go through the gap and turn left along the wall to the corner before crossing to the other side to find a clear path which ends at a road junction. Take the road opposite and at a fork go right to reach a stile/gateway on the left. Go over and along a farm road to pass through a second stile/gate. A short distance on, go right over a stile on to a clear moorland path leading back to the start point.

POINTS OF INTEREST:
The Roaches – A gritstone rock face much used by climbers. The name derives from the French, *Roche* meaning rock.
Lud's Church – A rocky chasm 200 feet long 60 feet high. Used for secret worship by 'Lollards', followers of religious reformer John Wycliff persecuted during the reign of Richard II. 'Lud' may derive from Walter de Ludank who held services here in the 14th century.

REFRESHMENTS:
None, you must take your own.

Walk 95   ILAM AND GRINDON   11m (17.5km)

Maps: OS Sheets Landranger 119; Outdoor Leisure 24.

A fairly strenuous walk, but with an easy finish.

Start: At 135508, the car park in Ilam.

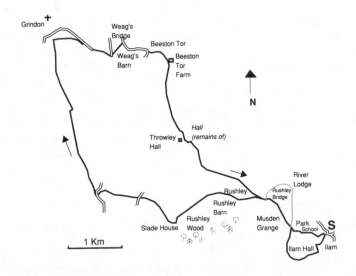

From the drive entrance to Ilam Hall take the road uphill and turn left, opposite the school, over a stile into the park. Follow the clear track, noting the ridges and furrows of the ancient strip lynchet cultivation system. Leave the track where it turns left and to continue to join another descending, right to a footbridge over the River Manifold. Cross the bridge and go right over a wall stile. Follow the easily seen way in a straight line via gate stiles to a road near Rushley Farm. Turn left as far as the bungalow drive and cross the adjacent stile. Climb the hillside, cross two stiles, (the second a ladder style) and follow the right boundary wall across two fields before going diagonally left to a corner stile in the next field. Cross and follow the left boundary through to Slade House passing, at a footpath junction, the remains of what was probably a lime kiln. Short of the house, follow the waymarked path diversion right on to and along a track to two small pools by a stile/gate. Cross and go diagonally left across the field to the corner stile and road. Go over the stile opposite, along the boundary wall and over another stile to follow the rough path descending steeply to the valley bottom past Lee House. Cross the footbridge over the River Hamps on to the Manifold Trail (see Note to Walk 17).

Go through the kissing gate to the left before turning right to follow the clear track uphill. Go left where the track ends, along the field boundary to and through a small gate in the corner. Turn right and follow a gently curving path over several stiled/gated narrow fields to reach a narrow road. Follow this to the right, through a farmyard and gate. Go left to another gate at the bottom of the hill. The path beyond, goes right, then left on a steady ascent, along field edges – ignore the farm track met part way along, stay with the hedge on your left – to **Grindon**. The Cavalier Inn (usually closed midday during the week) is a short distance up the road to the left. Go right to follow the road downhill round a sharp left hairpin bend and cross the stile immediately on the right. Descend the field parallel to the right edge, veering left near the bottom to pass through the hedge and over a stile to the Manifold Trail at Weag's Bridge. Turn right along the trail and follow the river to its confluence with the River Hamps (see Note to Walk 63) close to Beeston Tor, a 200 feet high limestone cliff favoured by rock climbers. A footpath sign (Throwley) points the way up the hillside on a rough track which is followed through a gate to a stile. Climb the field beyond past the terraces to a wall stile just left of the trees. Descend the field beyond to Throwley Hall Farm seen below, passing, on a stiled path, through the small spinney adjacent to the farm buildings and into the yard. Turn right, go through the gate ahead and on to the road swinging left to pass the old hall (1603) ruins before steadily descending to Rushley Farm. * From this point, reverse the outward journey as far as the footbridge. Go over and right across a stile on to Paradise Walk. The 'boil holes' near the path are where the Hamps and Manifold rivers emerge. From Ilam Hall take the path past the church back to the village.

*An alternative, slightly longer, return route follows the road across Rushley Bridge and round the right hand bend to River Lodge. A concessionary (toll 1p) riverside path goes from the Lodge to Paradise Walk.

POINTS OF INTEREST:
Grindon – The village church is known as the *Cathedral of the Moors*. It was built in 1831. Inside are two Saxon stone coffins.

REFRESHMENTS:
The Cavalier Inn (on the right day), Grindon (tel no: 05388 285).
Tea Rooms (in season) Ilam Hall.

Walk 96   **TRYSULL AND CLAVERLEY** $11^1/_4$m (18km)

Maps: OS Sheets Landranger 138 & 139; Pathfinder SO 89/99
& SO 69/79.

A good walk with panoramic views.

Start: At 851938, near the school, Hunters Green, Trysull.

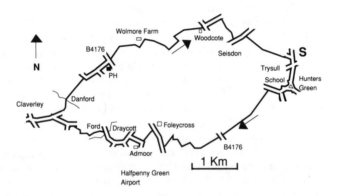

Go left along the road to Crockington Lane. Turn right for about 350 yards, to a
footpath sign on the left (Bridgnorth Road 1mile). Go over the fence in the hedge gap
and cross field on a bearing of 220° to the remains of a hedge. Go across to the
obvious holly tree in the next hedge. In the next field walk towards a solitary tree
(bearing 240°) bear the protruding corner of a hedge with a gap. Go through and
along the left hedge to a broad, green lane. Opposite, and slightly left, is a gap in the
hedge. Go through forwards to a pole ahead and keep on the same line to reach the
B4176. Turn right and then left on a track waymarked as the Staffordshire Way.
Ignore the next Way sign, going past a white house and on to a T-junction. Turn right
and follow a track to a road. Go right to reach an isolated building at Foleycross and
a green lane on the left. Follow this to Admoor Cottage. Go right along a lane to a

T-junction. Go left through Draycott to where the lane goes sharp left near a half-timbered building. Go ahead along a minor lane to a bend and a culverted stream marked as a ford on the OS map. At 12 paces from the culvert, take the iron fence on the left and use the steeping stones for the first few yards of marshland. On higher ground, follow the stream for a short way, then climb right to a hedge and telegraph poles. Follow the hedge and poles to a stile/gate. Follow the hedge to the right to a pointed, high corner of the field. In the corner cross a stile and follow the left hedge to the road. Turn left into the centre of Claverley.

Retrace your steps back as far as a letter box in front of two old cottages (Nos. 8 and 9). Go left through a small housing estate, until the road narrows to a track. Take a path crossing the Danford, a hedged path that widens and joins the elbow of a lane. Continue to the B4176 and the Woodman Inn. Cross the road to follow the signed footpath ahead, with the hedge on your right, to a stile. Go over the stile and half right aiming for the pole half way up the slope. Continue on the same line to reach a hunter's gate on the ridge top. Go through and through the one immediately behind it to the corner of the barn, and then left to a gate on to the Wolmore Farm drive. Turn right, ignoring the hedged track to Moat Rough, to reach a hunter's gate and a Staffs Way sign on the left. This path is a diversion from the original and as such is not marked on OS maps, however it is well signed and easily followed as far as the road near Woodcote. Follow the path and at the road turn left for a few yards and then right along Post Office Road for some way until reaching a stile on the right opposite house No. 148. Go over a stile, and two more, and follow the distinct path along the bottom of gardens on the edge of Seisdon. Do not be perturbed if you appear to be in someone's garden, you are on the right of way. The path continues to the last house on a bend, where a stile on the left reaches a minor estate road. The path goes directly across and through a garden to the road near the Smestow Brook bridge. If the way is blocked divert right, left and left – all in a very short distance – to reach the bridge. Continue along the road from the bridge to reach a green lane on the right alongside a house named 'Atlast'. This lane will bring you to The Mill, The Bakehouse and a road in Trysull. Go right, cross the road by the church, and continue to the school and Hunters Green.

Walk 97   **MONYASH AND MIDDLETON**   12m (19km)

Maps: OS Sheets Landranger 119; Outdoor Leisure 24.

A long, but not a strenuous walk.

Start: At 128659, Sparklow car park.

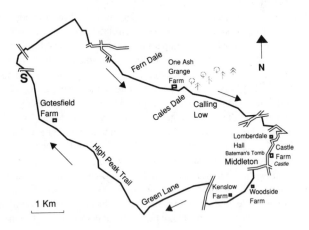

From the car park entrance cross the road to reach the High Peak Trail. Look for the field walls, and half way along the second field go right on to a path which inclines left to cross four small fields to the A515. Go right for a few yards, pass the Bull i' the Thorn Hotel (reputed to date from 1472), then go left on to a grass track, called Hutmoor Butts, very straight and a mile long. At the end there is a junction of tracks. Turn right on a track to the road to **Monyash**, which it meets at a sharp bend. Follow the road to the village. At the crossroads turn right along the road, past the pond, to reach a bend. Here go left on a track to a small valley. (Fern Dale). Across this dale the path forks: take the left-hand path which follows a wall, crosses it near a pond, and leads to the drive of **One Ash Grange** Farm.

 Follow the drive and turn left between the barns, as directed by a sign. Go over the stile at the end into a field. Go down the field, and at the rock outcrop follow the

ILAM AND ALSTONEFIELD

aps: OS Sheets Landranger 119; Outdoor Leisure 24.
Grand Tour of the area.   12m (19km)
art: At 135508, the car park in Ilam.

Wetton Brook Lodge Alstonefield
Church Farm
Wetton Hope Hall Farm
Low (322m) Green
Farm Milldale
Bincliff Mines (disused)
Highfields Mine (disused) Dove Holes
Ilam Upper N
Rock Taylor's
Wood Pickering
Castern Castern Tor
Hall Air Cottage
Ilamtops Dovedale Wood
Farm
Abbot's Rushley
Bank Bridge Bunster Hill
St Bertrams
Musden Wood Well
Ilam
Ilam S
Hall

1 Km

e the road left, past the memorial to a Mrs Walls Russell to find a footpath sign
ove Dale) and a gate. Go through. Ignore the Dove Dale path going right and take
track going left of the hill. This becomes a clear path along a boundary wall,
sing St Bertram's Well (ignore the stile on the left) and climbing steeply to a
ner stile on the left, partly hidden from view by a tree. Go over and take a diagonal
across the field. Go through the second gate on the left to a wall stile just left of a
n. Go over and turn left, then right on a track which passes through Air Cottage
unds (concessionary way) to reach a ladder stile by Dove Dale wood. Follow the
ar, but narrow, path through the wood as it wends down to the river at Ilam Rock,
isolated pillar of limestone. Turn left for a delightful walk on an easy path which
ows the river before ascending fields for a final short, steep descent into the pretty
let of Milldale near Viator's Bridge (see Note to Walk 41). Take the lane (Millway

204

rough path down into Cales Dale. Soon you will see a stile down a short path on the right. Go over it to reach a steep flight of steps up the other side of the dale. At the top is a stile: most folk cross and flop down on the grass to get their breath back.

Go up the field to a stile in a wall, then keep the same line, aiming for the buildings of Calling Low. At the farm go through a gate and follow the drive. At the far side bear right across a field to its top right-hand corner by a small wood. Cross the corner of the wood, then keep roughly the same line, there are waymarkers, to reach a road. Cross and walk along the right fork to Moor Lane car park. Turn right through the car park, then right down the path. Soon it bends left and goes down to a road: go left on the road, round the bend, then right on a short path by a wood to another road. Turn right and walk to a sharp bend. Just around the bend, go left down a track through a wood into Bradford Dale.

By the river cross the bridge and go right along the dale. At its end, follow the track up to **Middleton**. At the road turn right for a few yards, then left at the wide central area and left again up a road. Soon you find a wood alongside the road and by it a track going left. Take this for about $^3/_4$ mile to a junction. Bear right on the track to Kenslow Farm. Go left and right through the farm, then straight on to a road. Turn right for about a $^1/_3$ mile to a junction. There go left on a track, called Green Lane, which rises gently. At the top, by a line of trees, you cross a Roman Road, before gently descending to the High Peak Trail (see Note to Walk 28). Turn right on to the trail for an easy $3^1/_2$ miles walk back to Sparklow car park.

POINTS OF INTEREST:

Monyash – Once a centre of lead mining with its own Barmoot Court.
One Ash Grange – A monastery farm and house of correction for naughty monks.
Middleton – Once had a castle though there is little left to see now. The tomb of Bateman, who excavated many tumuli in the Peak District, is also here. He used brawn and shovel, and his diggings now appear more like vandalism than real research.
Green Lane – Referred to in an early 13th-century deed as the main route from Hartington to Middleton.

REFRESHMENTS:

The Royal Oak, Sparklow (tel no: 0298 83288).
The Bull i' the Thorn, Sparklow (tel no: 0298 83348).
The Hobbit, Monyash (tel no: 0629 812372).

Walk 98 Longnor, Hollinsclough and Pilsbury 12m (19km)

Maps: OS Sheets Landranger 119; Outdoor Leisure 24.

An invigorating walk through diverse scenery with many historical associations.

Start: At 088649, the Market car park in Longnor.

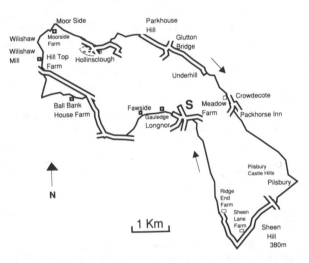

Head due west out of Longnor (see Note to Walk 83) and follow the footpath to Fawside. Go down and across the River Manifold to meet a road. Turn right for 0.5km, then go right, just after crossing the river again, along a lane. A steep climb for 0.5km leads to a turning, left, to Ball Bank House Farm. Continue past the farm and down the slope to the river and a footbridge. Go sharp right here and up the hill to the road. Cross this road for Hill Top Farm. Pass the farm and continue in the same direction for Willshaw. Turn right and down at this point and make for Moorside Farm. From the back of the farm take the track towards the river turning right to make for **Hollinsclough**. At the road junction in Hollinsclough go left towards Longnor for 0.5km then left down a farm lane to meet the River Dove. Cross the river and turn right along the track to meet the road to Glutton Bridge. At Glutton Bridge turn left

and almost immediately right and follow the lane to meet the green [...] Underhill. Cross the green lane and go over stiles to **Crowdecote**. Pass th[...] Inn and turn left down a lane. Follow the lane through fields for 2km to th[...] **Pilsbury Castle**. Take the lane down right to Pilsbury. Cross the Riv[...] head up the bank to the road. Cross the road and take the lane down for 1[...] Lane Farm where you turn right for Ridge End Farm. At Ridge End [...] footpath that follows the right bank of the River Manifold back [...] approximately 2km away.

POINTS OF INTEREST:

Pilsbury Castle – The Motte and Bailey remains of a Norman Castle.

Hollinsclough – The packhorse trail and bridge close to the village are o[...] route from Liverpool. Silk buttons were made in the area.

REFRESHMENTS:

The Cheshire Cheese, Longnor (tel no: 029883 218).
The Crewe and Harpur Arms, Longnor (tel no: 029883 205).
The Horseshoe Inn, Longnor (tel no: 029883 262).
The Packhorse Inn, Crowdecote (tel no: 029883 210).

Lane packhorse way) between cottages which climbs steadily to Alstonefield (see Note to Walk 41.

Pass in front of *The George*, a 16th-century coaching inn and go left, then right past the car park and toilets. About 100 yards beyond the road junction turn left down a track by a cottage. Go over a stile at the end and follow the boundary wall to go over two more stiles on to a narrow lane. Follow the lane, right, to a sharp bend and there turn right over a stile on to a green lane. About 150 yards along, turn left over a stile at a field corner and go diagonally right across two fields and stiles. Go ahead to a short section of wall and a corner stile at far end. Go to the far right corner and road T-junction. Take the left arm of the T to arrive in Wetton opposite the pub. (See Note to Walk 85.)

Turn left then first right to a barn on the left after first passing the car park and toilets. Cross the wall stile by the barn and another at the top of the field just beyond a large tree. Descend along the field boundary beyond and across the lane at the bottom. The hill to the left is Wetton Low with it's 16th-century BC burial mounds and 20th-century AD trig. point. A clear path ascends and traverses the hillside ahead, from which there are excellent views of part of the Manifold Valley and moors beyond. Follow the hillside path, past the remains of the Bincliffe and Highfields lead mines to where it ends at a wall corner. Cross the stile and turn left for 60 yards to a gate. Turn right to follow a broad grassy path to the gate/stile in the far right corner. The way ahead is clearly seen through successive gateways/stiles to the access road adjacent the late 18th-century Castern Hall. Go along the road past the Hall, leaving it at a small heap of sand and gravel to take a short cut over a stile and round the slope to rejoin the road. A few yards further on leave the road on a path angling down the field in a direct line for Rushley Bridge, seen ahead. The sole stile to negotiate is obscured from view by the small group of trees. Cross the bridge and in 50 yards turn left over a stile, to reach a wall stile. Go over and up the small slope. Go through the gate ahead from where the way ahead is easily seen, crossing the river by a footbridge. Turn right to cross a stile on to Paradise Walk a delightfully scenic path to Ilam Hall (see Note to Walk 78). Near the end are the 'boil holes' where the rivers Hamps and Manifold emerge from their underground routes. From the Hall take the path past the church back to the village.

REFRESHMENTS:
The George, Alstonefield (tel no: 033527 205).
The Old Royal Oak, Wetton (tel no: 033527 287).
Tea Rooms (in season) Ilam Hall.

Walk 100   **KIDSGROVE CIRCULAR**   13$\frac{1}{2}$m (21.5km)

Maps: OS Sheets Landranger 118; Pathfinder SJ 85/95 & 84/94.

An easy walk, with interesting, mainly urban, scenery.

Start: At 839544, the car park in Meadows Road, Kidsgrove.

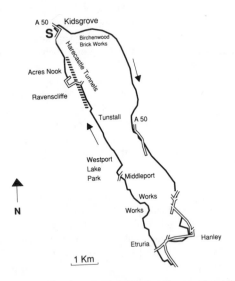

From the car park, turn right into Station Road and cross the A50 on to some spare ground to reach the track of the former Potteries Loop Line. Turn right on to this disused railway and follow it through the remnants of Birchenwood Colliery, gently arcing to the right, passing under Colclough Lane and continuing as the track eventually becomes the landscaped Tunstall **Greenway**. Cross Furlong Road and continue through a cutting until Scotia Road (the A50) is reached. Turn left along this road and then take the third turning on the right (an unnamed minor road). Turn left from this, back on to the Greenway, which recrosses Scotia Road and becomes the Burslem Greenway. Follow this until its junction with the A53 (Lee New Road). Turn right on to this road and then left at the traffic lights on to the A50 (Waterloo Road). Walk down the hill and rejoin the Greenway on the right, immediately after Winifred Street. This ends at Chelwood Street. Turn left on to this street, then left again on to Century Street.

Follow Century Street, which forks right, until its junction with Marsh Street and there turn right. At the traffic lights, on the outskirts of Hanley, turn right on to Etruria Road (the A5010). Shortly afterwards, turn left into the Clough Street Car Park roundabout on the A53 (Etruria Road). Turn left along Etruria Vale Road (the B5046) and right on to Bedford Street at the top of the hill. Cross the bridge over the Caldon Canal, turning right and then left on to the left bank of the **Trent and Mersey Canal**.

At the first bridge ahead, cross the road (the A53) and switch on to the right bank. Continue along the towpath until the **Harecastle Tunnels** are reached after approximately three and a half miles. Ascend the steps between the two tunnels and turn right, on to Chatterley Road. Turn left along this road and at the junctions ahead, bear right on to Hollywall Lane and then immediately left on to Boathorse Road (which is not signposted). At the gypsy site, this becomes a track. At the junction at the top of the incline, turn right (on to Acres Nook Road) and continue straight ahead down Nelson Bank and along Boathorse Road. At the junction with The Avenue, turn right and second left to Meadows Road and the car park.

POINTS OF INTEREST:
The Greenway – The dismantled Potteries Loop Line has been converted into this pleasant walkway, with interesting semi-rural and urban views.
The Trent and Mersey Canal – This was constructed by James Brindley and opened in 1777. Close to the junction with the Caldon Canal there is a Heritage Museum.
The Harecastle Tunnels – The original tunnel (on the left), which was constructed by Brindley, is disused and the canal now passes through the Thomas Telford tunnel, opened in 1827.

REFRESHMENTS:
The Harecastle Hotel, Liverpool Road, Kidsgrove (tel no: 0782 784196).
Rendezvous, 67 Etruria Old Road, Etruria (tel no: 0782 279330).
The China Garden, Festival Park, Etruria (tel no: 0782 260199/261450).

TITLES IN THE SERIES

Cheshire

County Durham

Derbyshire

Gloucestershire

Lancashire

Northumberland

Staffordshire

Wiltshire

Yorkshire (Vols 1 and 2)